Transform Silos
To Pillars

Transform Silos

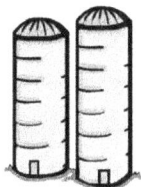

To Pillars

Moving from
Hate to Help

David Porter

T
TapCore
Publishers

Kansas City, Missouri

ISBN-10: 0-692-94074-X
ISBN-13: 978-0-692-94074-7

Published by TapCore Publishers, Kansas City, MO

Printed in the United States of America

FIRST EDITION

Dedication

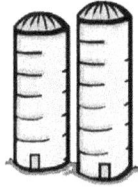

To Three of my Pillars:

My Mom - Marge Porter (1933-1989)
Who taught me about doing and caring for others and
pursuing every challenge.

My Dad - Tom Porter (1927-2014)
Who taught me a work ethic and implacable integrity I
can only hope to emulate.

My Wife - Lydia
Whose love makes me better every day.

Table of Contents

PART 5 – HOW TO WEAVE

TAKE ACTION

Forward

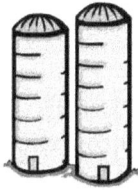

I first met David Porter back in 2014. To be frank, I was ready to be thoroughly intimated. After all, have you read his LinkedIn profile? Besides being a hugely respected lawyer (yes one of those) he also protected the interest of a large, US-based laboratory company in his role as a senior executive responsible for its corporate compliance, legal, quality management and enterprise risk functions.

David has over 25 years of experience working with businesses as a lawyer and business consultant. Before joining the laboratory company, he spent nine years serving as Assistant General Counsel for a Kansas City healthcare system. And he holds a law degree from Notre Dame Law School.

I already knew all this of course when he signed up for our CPP Master's program in Colorado; so yes, I was fearful. This would be no ordinary training and I fully anticipated every argument I made to be challenged, cross examined and effectively torn to shreds by an intellect way beyond my own.

How mistaken I was. Oh, yes, he did challenge, probe, and incisively question my case for enterprises to move 'Outside-In' and embrace the customer. What I discovered, however, was a deeply passionate guy who got it from the get go, and then pushed the logic even further. It was less a sparring match and more a meeting of minds – a common agenda to create a better model of business that helped employees, customers, owners, and shareholders.

Interestingly, however, David initially appeared to take an opposite view to my own. His belief that silos are not just a necessary evil of organizations, but could be the very essence of immediate and future success set me back somewhat. After all my experience as a best-selling author and senior executive with Citibank and then working with several of the world's leading corporations including Apple, Google, Bentley, Disney, and BMW suggested something altogether different. David's apparently contrarian view to my quest of smashing silos was intriguing and ultimately led to him sharing those insights, learning, and application with you in this book.

If then you too, like me, have felt oppressed and disconnected by silo thinking and practice then this book is indeed a remarkable contrarian revelation.

With concise and entertaining logic, you will be driven on a journey that turns on its head so much of the progressive modern business thinking (to destroy the silo) in our quest to get closer to the customer. Presenting a pathway to transform the mismanaged silos, you will explore the pragmatic arguments of optimizing, improving and overhauling them to become pillars of operational and strategic excellence. Something through which a corporation could become truly customer-centric in a world of turmoil and ever increasing complexity.

I am very proud to be able to call David a friend and colleague (even though he still rigorously challenges my every argument!).

Prepare now to have your world shaken and potentially change the way you think of business and customers forever.

Steve Towers

CEO, BP Group
London, August 2017

Introduction

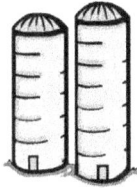

"The first thing we do, let's kill all the lawyers"

- William Shakespeare, <u>Henry VI</u>

Lawyer . . . the word creates a host of feelings – most not positive. I wanted to be a lawyer from the time I was 16 years old. The learning challenged me. The rigor of making a good argument intrigued me. I was not prepared for how the role, which I perceived would be respected, was not.

When I was graduated from law school, I looked forward to positive working relationships with clients. How could it be different? After all, I was being hired to help. My experience was quite the opposite. I discovered clients hired lawyers to get them out of trouble. They viewed them as a "necessary evil" to get from where they were to where they wanted to be. Phrases like "hired gun" and "professional mouthpiece" were the norm.

And the lawyer jokes . . . they are an entirely different story. Far from the idealistic "arm in arm" partnership I envisioned, the client engagement was one of necessity -- and not a positive necessity.

Early on this bothered me. My legal education included the true, albeit self-indulgent, "protectors of the system" rhetoric. We believed upon completing law school and surviving the gauntlet of the bar exam, we would be initiated into the hallowed role we envisioned.

For a decade I served my legal "apprenticeship" in private practice. I worked with many brilliant, self-effacing professionals. They gave me glimpses into what I hoped to be as a lawyer -- a trusted advisor. In *The Godfather*, Vito Corleone (played by Marlon Brando) called it, a *consigliere*. In my mind, I believed (and still do today) great leaders need a consigliere. I wanted to be that trusted advisor to a leader who was fighting the good fight.

The Foxhole

The chance to begin pursuing my vision in earnest came when I became Assistant General Counsel for a Kansas City healthcare delivery system. Now, I thought, the situation would certainly change because now I was one of them. I worked for the company. I was no longer a hired gun from the outside being paid on an hourly rate.

I was wrong. Despite being in the same company, I was far from being on the same team. I still carried that same descriptor -- lawyer. The barriers were still there. There were greater opportunities to try and break down those barriers. But, the fact the barriers were there surprised me.

My perspective changed forever after a conversation with my uncle. He was an executive with Lucent Technologies. He spent his entire career in the telecommunications industry working for a number of the AT&T family of companies before ultimately retiring from Lucent. One day we were discussing my move to an in-house role and in three sentences he crystalized how I could make the barriers go away: "Business people don't want to work with lawyers. They want partners. Make sure you stay in the foxhole with them."

And there it was. Those three sentences filled the gap in my thinking. I had previously understood my role was to advise my clients and let them execute. What I missed was that I could (and should) provide my advice within a connected relationship rather than from an outsider's perspective. Those three sentences became my professional mantra.

Roadmap to this Book

Those sentences also are a catalyst for this book. For over a decade, my focus has been on the broader area of compliance with legal work being a portion of my responsibilities. Increasingly my work has expanded to include regulatory, risk management, information security, business continuity, quality and business process management. While clearly not part of Operations, these functions are vital to the level of excellence a company achieves.

Throughout the book, I refer to these non-operational activities that make up my work today as "Core Threads." Core Threads are elements of a business that provide context and depth to Operations. We'll talk more about Core Threads later in this book.

Interestingly, as my work expanded to include Core Threads, a surprising revelation occurred -- Operations people disliked Core Thread people in the same way they disliked lawyers. It was not the dislike that made the revelation meaningful. It was the understanding that it was the outsider status driving the dislike.

This book focuses on how to eliminate the outsider status. It teaches how you can help Operations achieve optimal execution by using a strong process environment interwoven with strong Core Thread infrastructure. This book is a nod to my uncle's three sentences: "Business people don't want to work with [Core Thread People]. They want partners. Make sure you stay in the foxhole with them."

We begin by exploring the challenges facing today's businesses from a performance perspective. Certainly, the markets demand greater and greater financial performance. In addition, there is an ever-growing demand for stronger Core Thread infrastructure. We lay the foundation that Core Threads are really compliance functions that i) regulators require; ii) customers demand and iii) executives and boards need.

Part 1 looks at the value of silos in a business. Operations and management often live in silos. Much has been written about breaking down silos in organizations to create better performance. This book takes a different view of silos for three reasons: i) silos are natural and inevitable; ii) silos deliver key performance elements and iii) silos deliver structure that supports the achievement of corporate excellence.

In **Part 2** we explore how Core Threads are layered on to operations/silos which results in dysfunction and reduced performance. We explore why two demands -- financial performance and Core Threads -- are undermined when silos are destroyed. We encounter "Pour Mentality" – the approach of merely pouring Core Threads over Operations – and how this philosophy distances executive leadership from the very Operations that produce business success.

In **Part 3** we go in the foxhole. We discuss how to create greater performance with a laser focus on process. Integration of Core Threads into operational process begins with process. We discuss "Dip Mentality", the antithesis to Pour Mentality, which fosters designing Core Threads into Operations rather than simply being layered on to Operations.

In **Part 4** we analyze the **Hub Leader**. The Hub Leader's focus drives the transformation of silos into pillars. We explore the Hub Leader's vision and skills to weave Core Threads with operational process to create success. The Hub Leader is the partner business people want in the foxhole.

In **Part 5**, we get tactical. After understanding the challenges and the solution at a strategic level, Part 5 discusses how the Hub Leader executes. We discuss assessing your organization's ability to transform. We discuss the lens through which all of this work must be done -- the customer. We uncover the approach that creates an Operations/Core Thread partnership that is sustainable and drives continual improvement. Lastly, we touch on how the Hub Leader executes change management to minimize disruption and get processes quickly to the new normal.

In the end, we provide you with calls to action. We want you to take the investment you made in studying this book and turn it into action. Your actions create return on your investment, strengthen your delivery and bring sustainable value to your organization.

This book focuses on integration. Namely, how can we effectively make the Core Threads part of day-to-day operations instead of an add-on? Thus, we do not discuss in substantive detail the Core Thread areas. There are those who have that expertise and a wide variety of resources on those specific topics. To augment our systems-level discussion, there are **Resource Snapshots** highlighting materials to strengthen your tool kit.

If you want to learn how to transform your silos into pillars and forever change your business (and yourself), then let's get started.

Cast of Characters

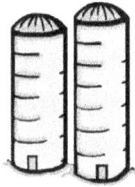

Before we dig into transforming silos into pillars, it is important to identify the cast of characters who are a part of this book. I introduce the cast at the beginning in the same way Hollywood used to in movies from the mid-twentieth century.

Thinking of old movies, I recall fondly a wonderful day I spent with my Mom in Cape Girardeau, Missouri at Southeast Missouri State University. I was in Junior High and participated in a state History Day contest. Mom was a parent chaperone on the trip. The contest consisted of writing and submitting a paper. Thus, there was no "competition" on the day we went to "Cape." It was more of an excursion.

When we arrived, most of my classmates went to arcades or other places to have fun on campus. My Mom and I went to an auditorium on campus and watched a Laurel and Hardy movie marathon. We both loved Laurel and Hardy and thought spending the time together laughing at their humor would be a wonderful day. It was.

I still remember the opening credits where you saw the people who were part of the movie: the cast, the writers, director, sound engineer and all the others were who made the film possible. I thought of that day as I put together the list below and hope it orients you to the characters and ideas that are part of your silo transformation journey.

Key Characters

- **Hub Leader**
  The Hub Leader is the star of our show. "Hub" is an approach, not a position. Anyone can be (and should be) a Hub Leader. Hub is a person who understands the necessary integration and interdependencies within a highly functioning organization.

- **Operations Leader**
  The Operations Leader sits in the silo we want to transform into a pillar. "Ops" is focused on getting things done for customers. Ops does not particularly care for Hub. They are often in conflict. We will explore how that conflict can be overcome.

- **Executive Leader**
  The Executive Leader holds a corporate position and has responsibilities across multiple silos. Hub usually reports to or has direct responsibility to "Exie." Exie wishes Ops would be more of a team player across the organization. Exie likes Hub but sometimes struggles with giving Hub enough

authority to transform Ops' silo. We will see how Hub can help with that challenge.

Key Concepts

- **Core Threads**
  Core Threads are the non-operational elements of a business such as compliance, quality, security, safety and continuity. Each business has its own set of Core Threads that strengthen the delivery of products or services to ensure customers are getting what they need.

- **Silo**
  There is a more formal definition of a silo later in the book. For now, a silo is any part of an organization that attempts to set itself apart from the organization as a whole for any purpose. Just like Hub is our star character, Silo is our star concept.

- **Layering/Pour Mentality**
  Layering is the process of Core Threads being added to Silo's work for the sake of the Core Threads. There is little, if any, focus on making the Core Threads part of the Silo's work. Rather, the Core Threads are simply extra work. This extra work is "poured" over the silo in an effort to get some level of adoption. This is what we call Pour Mentality.

- **Integrating/Dip Mentality**
  Integrating is achieved when Hub takes the time and effort to understand Silo's work and then make the Core Threads part of the delivery to the customer. This makes the Core Threads part of Silo's work, not something in addition to Silo's work. Integrating requires understanding what Silo needs and then providing it. The execution of Core Threads is a more precise engagement of each of Silo's pieces to "dip" them into the necessary Core Threads. This is what we call Dip Mentality.

So, there you have it. You know the key characters and have a flavor for the key concepts. The only thing to do now is get on the road to transformation.

Chapter 1

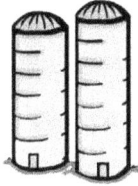

Requirements Continue to Rise

"The rate of change is not going to slow down anytime soon. If anything, competition in most industries will probably speed up even more in the next few decades."

– John Kotter, *Leading Change*

Technology is a fascinating concept. For many, the word technology means computer hardware, software and all other things that connect to or are identified with computers (or devices). Technology is much broader.

Webster's Dictionary defines technology as "the branch of knowledge that deals with the creation and use of technical means and their interrelation with life, society, and the environment, drawing upon such subjects as industrial arts, engineering, applied science, and pure science." In short, technology means the manner and

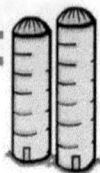

Resource Snapshot

How to be a Wildly Effective Compliance Officer
Kristy Grant-Hart

How to be a Wildly Effective Compliance Officer guides the reader how to bridge from the compliance chair to an effective relationship with those who have power in the organization. Grant-Hart provides clear, practical advice on going from a compliance officer to a business asset.

Key Quote

"Ideally, you want to connect with, and obtain buy-in from, both the people with named power and covert power. People with covert power who believe in your compliance mission will carry compliance ideas into their meetings and processes."

Website

www.compliancekristy.com

Why this Resource?

Compliance programs are largely the same in process and design as other Core Thread programs. Grant-Hart's strategies work for the Hub Leader as well as Core Thread program leaders.

www.silostopillars.com/resource-snapshot

means by which things are done -- computers or not.

Note the three key components of the technology definition: creation, use and interrelation. Businesses are constantly looking to create technology. From research and development divisions in vast multinational corporations to startups in garages around the world, the pursuit rages to create the next great technology.

Once the technology is created, the focus shifts to how the technology is used in the current environment and adapted to create the next technology. Technology creators must also navigate the challenge of interrelation. How does this new technology interrelate with other things in its economic ecosystem? Does it interrelate at all? Does it fundamentally change the entire ecosystem?

The creation - use - interrelation paradigm is not new. As technology advances, answering the three technology questions is more challenging. The onward advance of technology continues to provide the runway for continued evolution in business and life. Consider the following:

> *In my opinion, all previous advances in the various lines of invention will appear totally insignificant when compared with those which the present century will witness. I almost wish that I might live my life over again to see the wonders which are at the threshold.*

While we all would agree to this sentiment for the 21st century, this quote is from Charles Holland Duell, U.S. Commissioner of Patents in **1902**. Duell was correct about the 20th century and the decade and a half of the 21st century. The advances have been truly wondrous.

A simple example of advancing technology is recorded and distributed music. According to a 2004 PBS article,

Chronology: Technology and the Music Industry, there has been a continuing technology evolution within the music industry. These are a few of the highlights:

1877	Edison First Records Voice
1890s	Nickel Jukebox Gains Popularity
1900s	Music Recorded on Shellac Discs
1920	Radios in Commercial Production
1943	Vinyl Replaces Shellac for Discs
1964	Cassette Tapes Become Mainstream
1966	8 Track Tapes Enter the Market
1980s	Compact Discs (CDs) Enter Market
1990	MP3 Created
1993	Music Streaming Begins
2003	Launch of iTunes

Two things stand out in this list. First, technology is always moving forward. No matter how good the present idea or technology, there are people working on new ideas and new technologies. That effort alone creates a continuous propulsion to how things are done.

Second, technologies tend to evolve more rapidly with each successive generation. It took 40 years for music to go from shellac discs to vinyl. It took 13 years to go from MP3 to iTunes. Change is going to happen faster and challenge leaders to see what is next. This forward thinking allows leaders to be prepared rather than simply react.

It Never Gets Easier

Beyond the inevitability of change and the speed of change, it is clear that delivering in a business environment is only getting harder. According to the George Washington University Regulatory Studies Center, there were over 150,000 pages of U.S. Federal regulations in 2005. Most of these regulations apply to business

> Once the technology idea is created, the focus shifts to how the technology is used in the current environment and adapted to create the next technology.

environments and activities. By 2015, that number had risen to nearly 180,000 pages (a 20% increase). And that reflects only U.S. Federal regulation.

States within the U.S. as well as countries around the world are equally active in regulating companies in areas ranging from labor and employment to health and safety. Industry-specific rules create additional complexity and burden.

Beyond regulatory requirements, third party standards of conduct such as ISO and SOC 2 create additional requirements business operations adopt. So, while the world shrinks through global interconnectedness which makes global markets more available, it causes the challenges to grow in quantity and complexity.

Consider the example of data. In the healthcare industry, the lodestar of U.S. regulation is the Health Insurance Portability and Accountability Act ("HIPAA") which protects the privacy of and security measures applied to data.

Providers delivering healthcare within the U.S. alone not only must navigate the applicability of HIPAA data rules, they must also compare various U.S. state rules to HIPAA to determine which rules apply. For some issues, HIPAA governs. For others, the state law takes precedence.

The challenge is heightened because the rules change for one, the other or both. It is a constant effort to simply understand what rules are, let alone evolve processes to meet those changing rules. Those who handle data globally have an even greater challenge to integrate applicable international rules (such as GDPR) as well.

These rules present great risk to businesses because failure to adhere to them result in significant fines as well as reputational damage.

Increase + Complexity + Speed

The combination of increase in requirements, complexity of application and speed of change challenges business leaders. Beyond regulatory requirements, a separate set of requirements merits review -- customer requirements.

While the regulatory rules have a legal impact on businesses, customer requirements represent a parallel and equally important set of requirements that define your business' success. Some of these commitments are a product of the rules applicable to your client. Others are driven by the customer's risk mitigation strategies.

Because of the disparity in customer requirements, this book addresses customer requirements generically as a set of obligations that a sound business adheres to in delivering to its customers.

The need to identify and satisfy today's requirements and look down the road to tomorrow has never been more important. While many look to tool sets like Lean, Six Sigma, TQM or big data analytics, the core need is **insight**. Today's leader needs ways to better define the current state of business to evolve to future state in a way that is sustainable. From that foothold, the path to the horizon of tomorrow is achievable.

That foothold is embodied in a corporate structure that many see as the enemy of corporate growth -- the silo. The silo is one of our main characters. The insight tool for your business is the silo which you transform into a pillar of your company.

Think Compliance

As we move forward, Core Threads are the business elements we are trying to integrate into Operations. We call them Core Threads because they are the material we weave into Operations to build strength and sustainability. When we refer to the Core Threads as a company function, we refer to them simply as Compliance. Compliance? Yes, Compliance.

ISO standard 19600 addresses Compliance Management as part of the management system used to govern business operations. ISO 19600 focuses on "compliance obligations" (legal and regulatory-based requirements) and "compliance commitments" (voluntarily undertaken requirements, typically by contract) to make up the broader term of Compliance Requirements.

Nowhere in this internationally-recognized standard is there any focus on a particular set of requirements. Rather, the standard is designed as an umbrella to cover all requirements from all areas. Thus, Compliance makes a nice term for all the non-operational requirements placed on business areas. So, when we talk about Compliance or Core Threads in this book, it refers to the collective non-operational requirements that support the excellence customers demand and regulators require.

Effective compliance is a system within an organization. It originates from particular departments across the organization – quality, compliance, security, safety and continuity to name a few. As important as where compliance begins, it is important to understand where it is planted and grows. In short, it flourishes in Operations and Operations lives in silos. Next, we begin to understand why this maligned structure is, in fact, vitally important to an organization's health.

Part 1

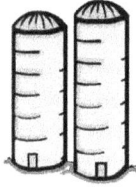

Silos are Natural
And Valuable

Chapter 2

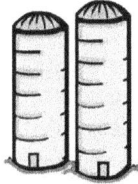

Silos Are Not the Enemy

"Why is it a good thing to break silos? All that happens when you break a silo is that the grain spills out. Or the missile falls over."

- Frankie Bow, <u>The Musubi Murder</u>

The silo is a reality. It is largely viewed as counterproductive to the successful operation of a business. *Business Dictionary* defines a silo as a "mind-set present in some company when certain departments or sectors do not wish to share information with others in the same company. This type of mentality reduces the efficiency of the overall operation, reduces morale, and may contribute to the demise of a productive company culture." Not a ringing endorsement.

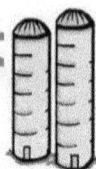

Resource Snapshot

The Silo Effect
Gillian Tett

The Silo Effect takes a critical look at the value and challenges silos present in an organization's success. Tett acknowledges the negative effect the separation and segregation silos cause. Equally, Tett outlines the benefits silos provide, <u>provided</u> the organization intentionally masters its silos.

Key Quote

"[A] starting point of this book is that the modern world needs silos, at least if you interpret that word to mean specialized departments, teams and places. The reason is obvious: we live in such a complex world that humans need to create some structure to handle the complexity."

Website

www.simonandschuster.com

Why this Resource?

The Hub Leader is a silo transformer. To be a transformer and deliver pillars in the organization, the Hub Leader would do well to read and absorb Tett's silo study.

www.silostopillars.com/resource-snapshot

Other themes for why silos are the enemy include i) silos stifle communication; ii) silos undermine the business' ability to execute comprehensive strategy and iii) silos don't let everyone see what everyone else is doing within the business. Despite these arguments, silos serve important interests in the success of a business. Among these are expertise, accountability and excellence.

Silos House Expertise

Business 101 teaches that a business is a group of people producing goods or services for profit. Steve Towers, CEO of BP Group and international expert on customer expectation management, argues that the only purpose of work in a business is to deliver "successful customer outcomes." The profits are a byproduct of those outcomes, not a purpose. Product/service delivery defines a business. Getting the delivery right on a number of levels (cost, speed, quality, etc.) is key to success. Delivery and execution are most successful when they reside in silos.

In his book, *Re-imagine!*, Tom Peters discusses businesses delivering exceptional products and services. Rather than a differentiator, Peters argues the delivery of great products and services is a given in today's market. It is a "ticket for entry" into the market. In Peters' own words:

> We believe that offering an excellent product or an excellent service is enough. Instead, we must understand that a "product" or "service" -- even an "excellent" one -- is but the "price of entry," the bare-bones beginning.

Customers presume your company delivers exceptional products and services. They assess your company to ensure their presumption is accurate. If that presumption is not accurate, the customer leaves. Without exceptional products or services, a business is not even in the game.

It is this need for sustainable execution that makes the silo valuable. Silos have the expertise to provide the type of delivery that keeps a business at the top of a market. Silos are the units that fully understand what is needed to succeed and delivers that excellent product/service.

Silos Ensure Accountability

An interesting catchphrase in business is "single throat to choke." It is the idea that when outsourcing some function or task or procuring a product or service, it is important to have some person or entity that is specifically accountable for the delivery. Silos provide that sort of accountability internally as well externally.

The silo defines internal accountability for delivery. While many talk about how silos keep others out, the silo defines itself by the things for which it is responsible. Thus, it keeps in the people who form the team that executes to a customer's satisfaction. That clarity of purpose is a valuable asset to be harnessed. The silo leaves no doubt within the organization who is accountable to deliver.

With this structure-driven accountability, organizational leaders can ensure successful outcomes are produced. There is no confusion regarding who is responsible. There is no mistaking who should have delivered.

The senior leader can monitor, manage and lead the fulfillment of whatever the silo should be doing. When there is a lack of clarity regarding who is responsible for something, the organization is at risk. As the pearl of business

> Customers presume a company delivers exceptional products and services.

wisdom reminds us, "what gets measured gets done." The silo contributes through the accountability it drives.

As discussed in Part 2 below, many silos are the face of the organization to customers. This creates the vital external accountability for customers. Through satisfied customers, a business has a sustainable success model. While some may view this external accountability as insular and divisive within the company, it is the foundation for long term customer relationships when managed appropriately.

Silos Drive Excellence

With the expertise and accountability for outcomes living in the silo, the third leg of the silo stool is excellence. Booker T. Washington defined excellence as "to do a common thing in an uncommon way." Every business team should hang that quote in their office and add "on behalf of the customer" to the end.

Excellence is nourished in silos. Again, the things that some identify as negative about silos -- separateness and exclusion -- drive excellence. Leaders within a silo are motivated by the fact they are a silo. They take pride in the work their silo performs. They are laser-focused on their services and products which further feeds into the silo's excellence. They inherently understand the silo shines a bright light on the team's performance. This motivates the leader and the team to ensure performance does not wane.

If there is no silo, excellence can be diluted. Corporate leaders have a span of control that is too broad to drive excellence to the front line in all areas. Within an effective silo, however, the focus is narrowed and excellence is more deeply ingrained.

With expertise, accountability and excellence in its DNA, the silo has much to offer. Far from being an enemy, the silo is the structure a forward-looking leader uses to produce continual improvement and sustainable results. That is, if the silo is designed properly within the organization.

Chapter 3

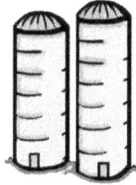

Silo Design is Important

Design is not just what it looks like and feels like. Design is how it works.

- Steve Jobs

Silos are not the enemy if they are designed and positioned properly. In fact, silos are a key ingredient to the continued growth and success of a business. Later, in Part 3, we discuss techniques to extract the most from these silos. But before that, it is important to understand silo design. This ensures that a silo is positioned to deliver value to the organization.

Understand a Silo's Deliverable

Evaluating a silo's deliverable is an important first step to determine if the silo is positioned for success. The

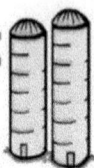

Resource Snapshot

Connecting Organizational Silos
Frank Leistner

Connecting Organizational Silos is a study in the work of Knowledge Flow Management (KFM) and increasing its value through use of social media. KFM is the systematic movement and exchange of information to keep organizations aware of the knowledge in the organization.

Key Quote

"Over the years I have changed my view on knowledge management and arrived at the notion of knowledge flows. I am convinced that knowledge is what exists in people's heads, but once it leaves their heads through speech or other content creation, it becomes information that needs to be absorbed and integrated with experience to create new knowledge."

Website

www.knowledge-management-online.com
/frank-leistner

Why this Resource?

Being able to effectively communicate the Core Threads work is vital to the Hub Leader's success. Leistner's book gives a practical, integrated strategy for that communication.

www.silostopillars.com/resource-snapshot

analysis keys on whether the silo has a "deliverable." Think of a <u>purpose</u> when considering deliverable. What undermines the deliverable is when a silo is trying to be all things to the customers it serves. Does the silo have a segregated, captive sales team? Segregated IT? Segregated anything beyond the silo's deliverable can indicate something needs to change.

If the answer to any of these questions is "Yes", there is likely design work to be done. In most cases, these non-deliverable functions are duplicative of the same functions that exist in other silos or at the corporate level. These duplicative functions are the catalyst for much of the negative silo literature.

The actual work within the silo, (i.e., the deliverable), should always be unique. It is unlikely a company has two separate areas that deliver the identical product/service to an identical customer base.

> *Trying to make all silos do the same things in the same way or have the same talents is a recipe for disaster.*

If you see the same functions in multiple places within the organization, there are delivery issues to address.

Identifying the deliverable and other things the silo is pursuing outside the deliverable begins a discussion on silo optimization. Much of the optimization centers on a renewed focus on the deliverable without distraction of other, non-deliverable areas. For instance, if additional and deeper IT resources can be brought to the silo from corporate, the silo has the opportunity to redeploy resources to have a more singular focus on its deliverable.

This singular focus then enhances the expertise, accountability and excellence discussed in the last chapter.

Do not take this evaluation lightly. You must be thorough and accurate. You must be prepared to propose and support any recommended pruning within the silo. It is almost certain the silo will resist. It takes a great deal of planning and discussion with the silo to achieve the needed pruning to bring greater focus to the silo's deliverable.

A key to the discussion is persuading Operations the pruning presents a better solution than the distractions within the status quo. If you want to transform silos into pillars of your business, do the work to convince the silo it is at its best when it is laser-focused on its deliverable.

Take Note How Silos Interact

After you understand and optimize the silos' delivery, the next step is understanding how silos interact. Studying your silos' interactions gives you more intelligence to transform your silos into pillars. Step one is determining if your silos interact at all. If there is no interaction, you need to open lines of communication and opportunities for interaction. This requires dialogue with silo leaders to understand why there is no connection. You need corporate leadership as an ally to initiate strategies for open communication and information sharing. The goal is to create a spark of interaction.

When there is even the slightest interaction, you need to foster and encourage it. An important strategy to encouraging interaction is understanding how the interaction takes place. Who are the leaders that foster the interaction? On what issue(s) do they interact? Do senior leaders within the silos know of this interaction? Do they encourage it? Do they fight it? Does it only take place with senior leadership direction or mandate?

Understanding the dynamic among silos gives a leader tremendous insight into how to work effectively with each silo. Strategies for improving silo interaction become apparent when you study and understand existing connections. Understanding who to engage and how to engage them becomes clearer. What is important and what is valued draws road maps for the leader to begin engagement and identify the road to success. These are the questions to keep in mind and apply during the discussion of the Hub Leader in Part 4.

Align Silos to Their Strength

Albert Einstein is attributed with saying, "everyone is a genius. But if you judge a fish by its ability to climb a tree, it will live its whole life believing that it is stupid." This idea is important when working with silos. All silos have strengths. There are things at which they excel and others which challenge them. Trying to make all silos do the same thing in the same way or have the same talents is a recipe for disaster.

As you are studying how silos interact, understand the topic(s) about which they interact. Are there particular things for which a silo is sought out by others? For instance, a particular silo may have an excellent record of implementing solutions on time and on budget. Others may be superb at crafting innovative solutions for customers. A third silo may be a rock solid steady performer that never misses a product or service delivery.

Noting these strengths helps create an understanding of the inherent culture these silos have created within and amongst themselves. Understanding the weaknesses with silos is also important. Just like our fish asked to climb a tree, understanding what silos cannot do helps avoid tasking the silo with the wrong things.

Think of a Major League Baseball manager. Each manager has a bullpen of relief pitchers. Some are right handed; others are southpaws. Some throw hard; others are crafty and use off speed pitches effectively. The good manager knows what his relief pitchers can and cannot do. That knowledge supports decision-making to bring in the right pitcher in the right situation to be successful.

Understanding the strengths and weaknesses within silos gives corporate leadership a leg up on managing the resources available. Like the interactions, silos' strengths and weaknesses give insight into how the leader can navigate amongst and with the silos with the greatest effectiveness.

Chapter 4

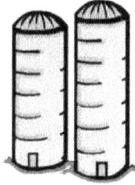

Silos Are Pillars in Disguise

"Opportunity often comes disguised in the form of misfortune or temporary defeat."

- Napoleon Hill

In the movie, *Dead Poets Society,* English teacher John Keating (played by Robin Williams) climbs on his desk and delivers a memorable lesson on perspective: "I stand upon my desk to remind myself that we must constantly look at things in a different way. Just when you think you know something, you have to look at in another way. Even though it may seem silly or wrong, you must try."

Leaders have varied business perspectives. The challenge is to understand each leader's perspective.

Resource Snapshot

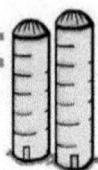

Tribes
Seth Godin

Tribes is a call to leadership. Godin believes each of us has a "tribe" that needs our leadership. He uses *Tribes* to motivate all to step into those leadership roles as we travel our professional and personal lives.

Key Quote
"Leaders have followers. Managers have employees. Managers make widgets. Leaders make change."

Website
www.sethgodin.com

Why this Resource?
As a Hub Leader, you are a leader. You work to transform the silos of widgets to the pillars of change. *Tribes* encourages you to take on your vital leadership roles to find success.

www.silostopillars.com/resource-snapshot

Silos Are Not Going Anywhere

A Google® search of "business silos" returns nearly 22 million entries in approximately a half a second. Not all 22 million entries were reviewed in the writing of this book. It is reasonable to conclude that the vast majority do not hold silos in high esteem. Loosely, the message of the nearly 22 million articles and entries related to business silos is simply "silos are bad."

Consider this. If there are nearly 22 million articles devoted to the topic of business silos, they must be everywhere. If the vast majority of writers conclude silos are

Leaders across all organizations have different perspectives on the business.

bad for business, would it not make sense that silos are a dying breed? The truth is, silos are as prevalent today as ever.

The continued existence of silos is attributable to one or both of two possible causes: 1) silos naturally evolve within an organization when human beings coalesce into working groups or 2) silos, despite their alleged negative reputation, bring some level of positive value to organizations.

This is where Mr. Keating rejoins the discussion. The challenge is to climb on the desk and see silos from a different perspective. Think of silos in a different way. Recalibrate your approach. The challenge is worth it because silos are real and they are not going away anytime soon.

Silos Even Look Like Pillars

At the beginning of each chapter there is an illustration of a silo. It is a tall, cylindrical structure. From the top of Mr. Keating's desk, we see more and different details. We can see the silo is designed to keep things in (grain, missiles, work teams) and to keep things out (rodents, dirt, Compliance staff). But wait. What other elements do we see? Rather than keep things in or out, could there be an additional use for a silo?

A silo bears a striking resemblance to another structure -- a pillar. And while we first see a silo is designed to keep things in or out, our view from Mr. Keating's desk gives us the broader perspective of the silo as a structure to provide support. A pillar holds things up. It provides a strong foundation. It causes structures to last – to be sustainable. Could a silo be such a structure? Yes. Silos become pillars by the work of a few, designed to help the many – advocated by leadership.

This is the premise from which the rest of this book proceeds. That thing you see as a silo, is also a pillar. It can, if you choose, provide support to an organization. It can, if you choose, be the mechanism to strengthen processes to ensure unfaltering delivery to the customers for whom businesses exist. It can, if you choose, be the lens through which you can gain a new found insight into your business and its performance. It can be the foundation for sustainable excellence.

If you choose.

Part 2

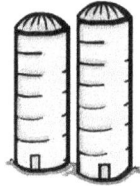

The Problem:
Layering Compliance on Silos

Chapter 5

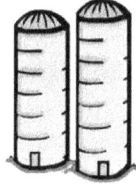

What Operations Does

"In the end, all business operations can be reduced to three words: people, product, and profits."

- *Lee Iacocca*

There are two fundamental elements used to define the health of a business -- revenue and expense. From these two measures a business' profit is calculated. We discussed earlier that profit is a byproduct, not a purpose. But it is an important byproduct. If there is no profit, there is no business.

Digging below the surface on the expense side of a business' ledger helps quickly identify Operations. There are two general categories of expense in a business: COGS and SG&A. COGS (Cost of Goods Sold) are expenses directly related to the production of the business' products and services. COGS includes things like raw materials, wages for people who produce/deliver the good or service, shipping, etc.

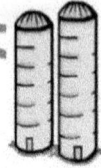

Resource Snapshot

Faster Cheaper Better
Michael Hammer and Lisa W. Hershman

Faster Better Cheaper is the last work from process guru Michael Hammer. In fact, Lisa Hershman finished the book after Hammer's death in 2008. Hammer and Hershman take a deep dive into how work gets done and expose the importance design has in the execution of that work.

Key Quote
"But the root cause of persistent performance problems is found not in who reports to whom but in how work itself is organized and performed."

Website
http://www.hammerandco.com/

Why this Resource?
Although a Hub Leader is not part of Operations, being versed in Operations is important. *Faster Cheaper Better* provides an education in Operations that allows the Hub Leader to weave the Core Threads consistent with a sustainable design of work.

www.silostopillars.com/resource-snapshot

SG&A (Selling, General & Administrative) are the indirect expenses of producing the business' products and services. SG&A includes things like cost of customer acquisition, utilities, and wages for people who are not directly involved in the production of the company's product or service, etc. It also includes all expenses related to Compliance.

The distinction identifies the two main teams within a business: Operations and Administration. For anyone who has worked in a business for any length of time, they may have heard Operations <u>versus</u> Administration. There can be a friction between these two groups because they see the business from their own unique perspectives. Each team feels the other does not understand who they are and what they contribute to the company's success. In many instances, they are correct.

Looking deeper, the friction may be rooted in the normal human desire for importance. Operations and Administration collide because each is trying to ensure its importance is understood and acknowledged by the other.

There may also be a much more practical reason for the friction. Operations is the breadwinner. It produces the product or service for which the company gets paid. Operations

> *When Administration layers, Operations resists.*

generates revenue and creates the company's identity based on its production of the things for which a company is known. You might characterize Operations' view as "without us, nothing gets made and the company would not exist."

41

Administration plays in a different space. Administration does things like hire people, sell goods and services to customers, ensure compliance, protect sensitive data, invoice customers and a host of other things. If Operations is the breadwinner, Administration facilitates the breadwinning. Administration ensures a wide variety of things are in place so Operations' work is optimized and, in some cases, even possible. You might characterize Administration's view as "without us, Operations cannot produce and the company would not exist."

Note the common thread between the two: without us, the company would not exist. That is a statement of importance. Few in either area of a company actually say this. It would be unseemly to do so in today's politically correct environment. But to think these feelings do not exist would be naive.

It is this competing for importance that triggers why Administration often layers requirements on Operations as we will discuss in Chapter 7. Consider the following examples:

- A compliance officer publishes a policy to meet a new requirement from the Food and Drug Administration (FDA). The new policy directs action that is largely inconsistent with how a product is currently produced. Operations has to invest tremendous effort redesigning the process to meet the compliance policy.

- An information security leader sends an email to Operations outlining a new data security protocol to be implemented to protect sensitive information. Operations must identify where this sensitive data exists in its processes and then perform redesign.

- A quality professional issues an internal audit report identifying gaps in an operational process that present unacceptable failure points. The report seeks Operations' plan to close the gap and reduce the risk present in the process.

Nothing in any of these examples is inherently wrong. People that work in compliance, information security and quality engage in these activities every day. They correctly believe that these activities are important to the company and deliver key elements customers expect.

The concern with each of the examples is the lack of engagement with Operations. Administration executes these actions and layers them on Operations. Operations is resistant to these activities and, in some cases, simply does not comply. When this occurs, gaps remain and customer needs are not met. In short, the company fails to meet its customer requirements.

Each example above is a classic "layering" failure. When Administration layers, Operations resists. Requirements are not met. Customers' needs go unmet. The company suffers.

These "layering" actions also negatively reinforce the company's silos. Layering increases friction and heightens the need for importance. That need for importance manifests itself in conflict and making everyone's job harder.

There is a better way. In Part 3 we explore integrating as an alternative to "layering" and learn why an integrated approach makes silos work more effectively. We discuss how integrating leads to designing Compliance into operational processes to make it a natural part of

Operations' work. The key takeaway here is to be keenly aware to avoid layering work on Operations.

Chapter 6

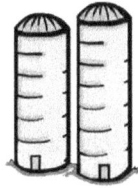

"Management" as a Silo

"Most of what we call management consists of making it difficult for people to get their work done."

- *Peter Drucker*

Typically, silo behavior is attributed to Operations. Administration is not immune to creating a "management silo" of its own.

Many avoid characterizing management as a silo. They do not believe there is a silo. With so much interaction with Operations, management simply cannot be a silo. The argument does not hold water.

Management's silo behavior is spawned from how management activities are planned and executed. In most cases, management makes decisions and creates plans among its own team without Operations being involved. There is little, if any, input from Operations. In short, the

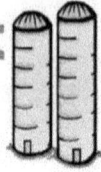

Resource Snapshot

Spanning Silos: The New CMO Imperative
David Aaker

Spanning Silos explores how Chief Marketing Officers (CMO) navigate among silos to break down the segmented and often inconsistent marketing messages that arise from decentralized marketing. One of the interesting elements is the identity of various roles CMOs can plan in executing on their integration objective.

Key Quote

"Too often, a master brand, perhaps even the corporate brand, is shared by many, sometimes by all, silo groups. Each silo is motivated to exploit the equity of the brand without any concern for the brand's role in other business units."

Website

www.prophet.com

Why this Resource?

Spanning Silos provides a real world view of executing a non-operational function (marketing) across multiple operational silos. This gives a great insight into how a Hub Leader can do the same with Core Threads.

www.silostopillars.com/resource-snapshot

foundation of the management silo is based on management's planning and execution that takes place without Operations being involved. These unilateral actions build the management silo walls. Operations resists. Management separates. Compliance seeks independence.

Resistance

One of the primary characteristics of a silo is resistance to oversight. In his book, *Spanning Silos*, author David Aaker offers an example of how silos can undermine attempts to centralize a key corporate function, namely marketing:

> *A CEO decides that the organization needs an empowered CMO (Chief Marketing Officer) with a competent supporting staff <u>to reign in the silo groups</u>. Whatever the reason, the CMO comes on board and aggressively attempts to make marketing more strategic and synergetic by creating an advertising campaign with a new centralized agency or redoing the brand vision complete with new logos and brand books. The result is a failure to achieve any of the objectives or even a dramatic flameout. In either case, the CMO leaves. <u>The silos have successfully repelled an attack on their autonomy and are free and clear for some time to come.</u> (emphasis added).*

Note Aaker's description. "[T]o reign in silo groups" highlights the CEO's true intention. The silos are not in step. They are not playing well in the corporate sandbox. They must be reined in. This is a management silo plain and simple. No collaboration or engagement. Just bring in the new CMO and get control of those unruly silos.

On the back end of the example, "repelled an attack" is the response to the management silo. This is classic resistance. Go back to the quote above. Who made the decision to consolidate? The CEO. Who is

> [T]he foundation of the management silo is based on the planning and execution that takes place without Operations being involved.

empowered to execute the CEO's decision? The CMO. Is there any engagement with Operations noted? No. In short, silos resist being "reigned in" from the outside.

The CEO and CMO planned and decided to do something to Operations. In such a case, siloed Operations do more than simply not engage with management. Silos often intentionally keep management out of their businesses through obstruction, lack of candor in reporting or obscuring business data to make oversight difficult, if not impossible.

Separateness

Corporate leadership has responsibility for a number of siloed operations. Corporate leadership is the body that is responsible to coalesce the work of a number of silos into a unified deliverable for the organization.

Given the number of operations for which management provides oversight, separateness is often sought. This separateness can be spurred by a number of considerations. Separateness helps avoid favoritism. No member of management wants to be seen as favoring one silo over another. Much like a parent does not want to play favorites among children, the corporate leader does not want to be perceived as playing favorites among business lines. They believe it will undermine their position across all business lines.

The problem is that separateness turns into disengagement. Once disengaged, the management silo is ineffective in providing the needed oversight. Management separates itself into its own silo with protection of its power base as a primary objective.

What results is an Operations silo that is more energized to protect its own power. Management retreats to its silo as well. Engagement is non-existent. Management and Operations have a politically correct, arm's length relationship. Progress is fought. Collaboration is out of the question. The company loses. Its customers lose.

Need for Independence

Many functions in management (e.g., finance, internal audit, compliance, quality) use independence as a crutch that fosters the management silo. For these functional experts, independence is believed important because they tie their effectiveness to being independent. If they do not remain independent, they are co-opted and lose their ability to keep the company on track. Or so they believe.

While the independence argument has some appeal, it is largely a restatement of the separateness argument. In essence, the argument is based on the premise that "unless it is us versus you, we cannot do our jobs. So, you stay in your operational silo and I'll come do what I need to do to you when it needs to be done. When we arrive, you will cooperate and that will be that." In short, independence is separateness wearing a subject matter shawl.

Is it any wonder there is a lack of cooperation?

You do not need to buy into the independence crutch. Your solution as a three-step process. First, ensure the professional autonomy needed to be effective. Autonomy does not mean separateness. It means standing firm in the things that are required. Second, offer assistance. Get on the inside, be of help and deliver value. Third, engender trust. Never allow your motives to be in question.

Recognize that silos exist both in Operations and Management. Action to address both are important throughout the transformation of silos into pillars. Just as the operational silos have value, so does the management silo. It is the Hub Leader's job to weave the core threads into each silo and across all silos to bring sustainable strength to the organization.

Chapter 7

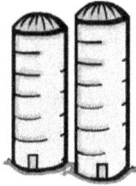

Pour Mentality

"The single biggest problem in communication is the illusion that it has taken place."

- George Bernard Shaw

What in the world is "Pour Mentality"? It does not sound like anything related to business. Well it is. Pour Mentality is what drives layering on Operations. It is an approach that simply pours requirements over Operations until the silo eventually "gets it" and aligns with management's plans. Few who pour understand that layering is not a recipe for success.

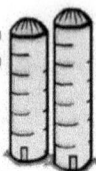

Resource Snapshot

Silos, Politics and Turf Wars
Patrick Lencioni

Silos, Politics and Turf Wars is part of Lencioni's long line of business and leadership fables. The book focuses on how colleagues become competitors because barriers arise through the creation of silos. Lencioni sets out a clear pattern to the silos and how executive leadership can overcome those barriers.

Key Quote
"In most situations, silos rise up not because of what executives are doing purposefully but rather because of what they are failing to do: provide themselves and their employees with a compelling context for working together."

Website
www.tablegroup.com

Why this Resource?
Lencioni's book focuses on the elimination of silos. Importantly, it also highlights that the core challenge lies in the design of work. Hub Leaders can find value in Lencioni's work to strengthen silo design rather than eliminate silos.

www.silostopillars.com/resource-snapshot

The best way to think about Pour Mentality is to consider a stack of pancakes. The stack is 3, 4 or 10 deep. They are beautiful. They are delicious.

What does the stack of pancakes also look like? That's right -- a silo and in this case, an operational silo. With its cylindrical shape and vertical profile it reminds us of that silo that exists in rural communities and businesses all over the globe.

The syrup represents the things management wants to layer on Operations in that silo: compliance programs to avoid trouble; quality programs to ensure our products meet standards; information security requirements that keep data safe from the bad guys.

Silo leadership, for reasons of protection, autonomy or resistance, absorbs most of the syrup and acts as an umbrella for the rest.

Looking more closely at the syrup in the picture the Pour Mentality flaw becomes apparent. The syrup is being poured on top of the pancakes in the same way Core Threads are poured over the top of silos. When you pour the syrup on the stack, the top pancake gets a bunch of syrup and the rest of the syrup falls over the sides and lands in the plate. Pancakes 2, 3 and beyond get virtually no syrup. They are largely dry and have not absorbed any of the sweet maple nectar that makes eating pancakes worth it. We should do something about that, shouldn't we?

Awareness Programs

Awareness programs are the most common response to Pour Mentality. Awareness programs arise from and are caused by Pour Mentality. Everyone has attended an awareness program. Some have even presented awareness programs.

The awareness program goal is to correct for Pour Mentality's critical flaw – namely, that pancakes 2, 3 and beyond did not get any of the syrup. By not getting any of the syrup, these parts of the silo are "flying blind" to achieve the Core Threads. Businesses all over the globe spend billions of dollars every year to put on these sorts of programs.

All awareness programs follow the same general outline: 1) this topic is really important; 2) it is important because (regulators, customers, management) expect it of us; 3) we expect you to believe this topic is as important as we do and 4) go out and apply what we have told you. Attendees can ask questions but there is likely not enough substantive information shared to trigger a meaningful question.

Staff members return to their areas and ask themselves "what was that and how does it apply to me?" When they ask someone in their silo management, they get some version of "don't worry about it; just do your job" as an answer. This happens because when the topic was poured out, it did not get to all the right people and the awareness program did not correct that problem.

Who Got the Syrup?

So who got the syrup? A whole bunch of syrup was poured. Where did it all go? The stack of pancakes reveals the answer. The stack mirrors the various levels within the silo with the silo leadership at the top (pancake 1) and the front line employees at the bottom (pancake 10). Managers and other staff are in the middle.

Much of the syrup was absorbed by silo leadership with the excess falling down the sides. Little, if any syrup got to any other layer. If the syrup was going to penetrate the silo, it would have to do so with the help of the silo leadership. But, the silo leadership is largely uninterested. Syrup pouring is a "layering" activity. It engenders indifference from most and outright resistance from the rest.

Silo leadership, for reasons of protection, autonomy or resistance, absorbs most of the syrup they must and acts as an umbrella for the rest of the silo staff. This ensures none of the others in the silo are distracted with having to absorb the poured syrup. They may have to attend an awareness session. But awareness causes far less disruption than being soaked with syrup.

Can the syrup get to the right place? Yes. We'll discuss that in Part 3. Know this. When the syrup gets to the right place, you have found the beginnings of the tapestry you can use to transform business silos into pillars.

pointed out, it did not go to all the right people and the awareness program did not correct that problem.

Part 3

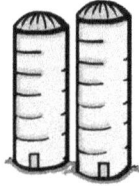

The Solution:

Designing Compliance

Into Silos

Chapter 8

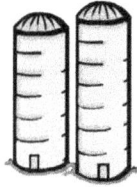

Why Silos Matter

> *"Every company has two organizational structures: The formal one is written on the charts; the other is the everyday relationships of the men and women in the organization."*
>
> *- Harold S. Geneen*

Organizations have structures.   Note the plural. There is often more than one structure in even the best of organizations. This is why we begin Part 3 by returning to the importance of silos.

If structure is an inevitable part of an organization, silos should be that structure. Chapters 2 & 3 explored why we should not eliminate silos because silos can be pillars. In this chapter, we more deeply look at the value silos bring to the structures within organizations.

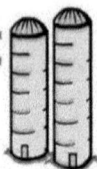

Resource Snapshot

Seeing Red Cars
Laura Goodrich

Seeing Red Cars takes the common occurrence of someone, after purchasing a red car, seeing more red cars than ever before and applies it to business and teams. The focus is on . . . focus. How you gain focus and how you execute after finding your focus. Goodrich breaks it down to a three-step plan of i) think it; ii) see it and iii) do it.

Key Quote
"Playing to our strengths . . . brings out the best in us. It's the kind of work we get lost in."

Website
www.seeingredcars.com

Why this Resource?
Part of the Hub Leader's work is to refocus others to think, see and do work differently. *Seeing Red Cars* is a simple and repeatable formula to make your Hub Leader work more effective.

www.silostopillars.com/resource-snapshot

Silos Foster Clarity

In his book, *The Advantage*, Patrick Lencioni identifies clarity as one of the key attributes of a highly functioning team. Clarity defines the purpose of the team, organization or silo. Clarity also offers those within those teams, organizations or silos a clear roadmap to achieve their purpose.

Properly designed and functioning silos are important tools in providing clarity. Silos do not intrinsically create clarity. Management cannot passively allow silos to exist. Unmanaged, silos do not create clarity. They create confusion because they act on their own missions, not the company's.

Silos create clarity when they are positioned and led as messengers of the corporate strategic objectives. Those objectives may be the work of corporate management; or, more optimally, those objectives are created in collaboration between corporate management and silo management.

When silos are positioned as carriers and catalysts of corporate goals, they drive strategic priorities in a way that is consistent with corporate priorities. The silo structure improves the achievement of corporate goals because the silo message drives those goals to the front lines, nearest to the customer.

This is where corporate leaders reach that pivotal decision; do we i) create corporate plans and deliver them to the silos or ii) collaborate with the experts in our silos to create plans that mesh across the entire organization? The fork in the road defines two modes of planning: i) planning that is layered on Operations and ii) planning integrated with Operations.

Planning layered on Operations is easier. No effort is needed to seek out and consider the input of others. Despite the relative ease of planning, execution is tougher, if not impossible. Silos will resist and obscure the plan, which destroys clarity. Corporate leadership will be pursuing a plan they devised and for which they can ultimately take credit. The silos are executing their plan. These cross purposes likely result in neither plan coming to fruition. Far from taking credit, corporate leadership will need to explain why their plan failed.

> *If structure is an inevitable part of an organization, silos should be that structure.*

Planning with Operations is harder -- much harder. It tests corporate leadership's talents. It takes more time, effort, patience and persistence. It is messy. It does not result in a plan that tracks what corporate leadership sketched out in advance. Flexibility and open mindedness are required. The plan is "ours" not "mine".

When planning is with Operations, silos buy in. They work toward achieving the plan because part of the plan is theirs. They have "skin in the game" which drives clarity of purpose within the silo and fosters clarity across the organization. In short, the more difficult planning with Operations results in optimized execution.

Silos Drive Outcomes

Silos drive the proverbial bus. Earlier we talked about how silos drive excellence in the organization. Here, we go further to identify why silos are, in fact, good for business.

The primary objective of business is to make and sell a product or service for a profit. While the objective is simple, it is not easy. New businesses show a high failure rate. A great idea for a product or service does not guarantee a profitable business. Some do, however, find the right formula for a great product or service that can be delivered in a profitable way to a dynamic and loyal customer base.

For those who find that formula, they need an Operations engine to produce that product and deliver that service. It is almost certain this production/delivery system has many attributes of a silo. We have discussed many such attributes: expertise, accountability and excellence. Silos do more.

At their core, silos are the revenue-generating engine of a business. They are not simply a group of people who serve at the behest of corporate management in producing a commodity that corporate sells. To the contrary, silos are that gritty part of the organization that gets the job done.

Engines make a good analogy for describing silos. Think of the vehicle you drive. When you look at it in your driveway you see its form and shape. You see its paint and profile. What you do not see is its engine. The engine is tucked away in its own compartment, under a hood. It can be accessed under that hood and it can be activated from the interior of the vehicle. It is largely unseen. Being unseen, however, does not diminish its importance. Take the engine from a vehicle and the result is a large, shiny paper weight. Take the silo from the organization and the result is no revenue which means no business.

The engine analogy carries through to one last point. Despite making the vehicle go, the engine is not invincible. It must be cared for. It must be maintained. This is equally true of the silo. Part of that care and feeding is weaving the Core Threads into silos to transform them into pillars. It is the Core Threads that enhance the operational processes to become sustainable drivers of corporate success. More to come on that.

Silos Are Identity

One would think that the fact silos drive the revenue that produces the success of a business would be enough to establish the silo's worth. That is not true. This final facet of silo value cements why silos are so important to the successful business. Silos are at the heart of a business' identity and brand.

Think of your favorite professional sports team. Your team has a number of players. It has a coaching staff. It has a large organization of people supporting those players and coaches. Despite all these people working with the team, virtually every professional sports team has a "face of the franchise." The face of the franchise can be a coach or an administrative person. But, in nearly all cases, it is a player.

The player is either the best player on the team or is the clear leader of the team. The face of the franchise speaks for the team -- officially and unofficially. When things are good, the face of the franchise is out front discussing the team's success. When things are not so good, the face of the franchise deals with that too.

Silos are the face of your company's franchise. While you have support departments and corporate leadership within your organization, who is it that your fans look to in good times and bad? Wait, what? Your organization does not have fans? Think again. If your business delivers goods and services to customers who are loyal and keep coming back and working with your company, you have fans. They may not come to a stadium and hold up foam #1 fingers. But your customers are your fans (or at least they should be).

So, back to the question, whom do your fans look to in good times and bad? That is right, the silo. The silo represents that face of the franchise for your loyal customers. By delivering outcomes, the silos are the embodiment of your company. The silo defines what the company is in good times and not so good times.

You certainly have people in the organization that work specifically on defining and establishing your company's brand in the marketplace. However, when the rubber meets the road between your business and your customer, it is the silo doing the branding. It is the kind of branding that sticks.

All in all, silos are an integral part of a company's success. They foster clarity within the organization. They drive outcomes. They are your company's identity. Silos matter. They need to be understood. They need to be cared for. They need to be worked with and not just layered upon by Compliance.

Once you accept the silo's value, you can identify the Core Threads to design into operational silos. This begins making them pillars of the business.

Chapter 9

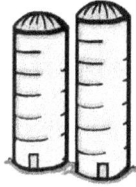

What Silo Walls Teach

"I love to think of nature as an unlimited broadcasting station through which God speaks to us every hour, if we will only tune in."

- *George Washington Carver*

Silos give us clues about what we should do to transform them into pillars. Our job is to spend the time to identify and understand the clues that will guide our path. The transformation we are pursuing involves integrating Core Threads into Operations to solidify the process of making products or delivering services.

Core Threads are customer requirements. Yet, they are not at the heart of Operations' workflow. Without focused effort, the Core Threads become activities that are simply layered on Operations. The result is the Core

Resource Snapshot

Change the Culture. Change the Game
Roger Connors and Tom Smith

Change the Culture. Change the Game is a tactical reference in moving organizational culture to align with success. Connors and Smith segment company "culture" into i) experiences; ii) beliefs; iii) actions and iv) results. The book then guides the reader to move each of the elements into sustainable alignment to successfully manage culture.

Key Quote

"Either you will manage your culture, or it will manage you."

Website

www.changetheculturechangethegame.com

Why this Resource?

Transforming silos into pillars is a game changer for the Hub Leader. Culture must align for this change to occur and be sustained. *Change the Culture. Change the Game* offers a crystal clear map to that successful change.

www.silostopillars.com/resource-snapshot

Threads being perceived as extra, non-value added work that can be ignored. The effective Hub Leader navigates beyond this challenge to reverse this non-value perception.

The clues to integrating Core Threads into silos are embedded in how silos are built. Silos are large round structures with very thick walls. It is the walls that cause the term "silo" to have a negative meaning.

As the Hub Leader approaches integrating Core Threads, those same walls are instructive how to achieve success. Understanding why the inside and outside of the silo's wall exists teaches the Hub Leader how to address the silo and successfully integrate the Core Threads to transform the silo into a pillar.

Keeping Out

The outside of the silo wall is designed to keep things out. The wall of the Operations silo is designed in the same way. The silo believes in its ability to execute. It is resistant to interference or even involvement from others. It relies on the silo to keep others out of its business.

As a Hub Leader wanting to weave Core Threads, you must acknowledge and accept this barrier. You do not have to like it; but, it is going to be there nonetheless. The resistance is intended to protect the silo from outsiders. Outsiders are a distraction that brings negative consequences to the silo.

Wanting to keep others out is a natural characteristic for Operations leaders because of their singular focus on execution. In their mind, outsiders only cause execution problems. The Hub Leader's challenge is to accept the outside wall as a natural barrier. This acceptance allows Hub Leaders to avoid undermining their efforts through applying fundamental attribution error to Operations' behavior.

In short, fundamental attribution error is a person's tendency to explain another's behavior based on internal factors and to underestimate the influence of external factors. In other words, the Hub Leader attributes Operations' resistance to bad intentions or being a bad actor. Fundamental attribution error overlooks the fact that the resistance is a natural response and has little or nothing to do with the Hub Leader.

So, what does the outside of the wall teach? It teaches patience and persistence. Working through silos means probing until the time is

> *The path to value begins with integration.*

right, due to circumstances or relationships, to initiate working with a silo leader.

Even when the time is right, it takes time to make the needed connection, earn trust and deliver value. Thus, the Hub Leader must be patient to begin and persistent to see the transformation through.

Protecting Within

Just like there are two sides to every story, there are two sides to every wall. While the outside of the wall keeps others out, the inside of wall protects those inside. The silo wall is no different.

The team working inside the silo is the silo leader's responsibility. The team executes consistent with the silo leader's direction and consistent with the silo leader's values. Consequently, the silo team is near and dear to the silo leader's heart. This protection of the team is an expected because the silo leader views the team as part of the silo leader's "business."

Like the outer wall, the inner wall teaches patience and persistence. Timing and tenacity are required to address the inner wall and connect meaningfully with the silo team.

The inner wall also teaches respect and care. While the outside of the wall is used to protect the silo leader's business, the inner wall is used to protect the silo leader's people. This is the difference between the scoundrel who damages your house and the fiend who attacks your family. We certainly protect our property. How much more do we protect our family?

The silo leader protects both the business and the people. Greater care, however, is directed toward the people. Thus, it takes the Hub Leader more than simple patience and persistence to have influence with the silo team. The Hub Leader must demonstrate respect for the people within the silo.

In addition to respect, the Hub Leader must also care for what the people in the silo do. When you stack respect and care on top of patience and persistence, the Hub Leader can scale the outer wall and not get trapped by the inner wall.

The silo wall lessons can be difficult for a Hub Leader. No matter how pure of intent or strong willed the Hub Leader is, the silo walls teach their lessons. They cause self-doubt and defeat in the Hub Leader's mind. When Hub Leaders face the silo wall lessons, they can continue or retreat. Retreat should not be an option. In moving forward, however, a pause can do some good.

When the Hub Leader gets buckled by the silo wall, a three-step plan can get you back on track.

1. **Anger.**
   It is OK to get angry. The Hub Leader is not immune from this healthy emotion. Hub Leaders deal with their emotions privately. They work through why they are angry. What has triggered this response? What actions (or inactions) of theirs has caused the circumstances that triggered the anger? Use the anger as a catalyst to improve your performance, not derail it.

2. **Disappointment.**
   Just like anger, disappointment is OK. Hub Leaders put themselves out there every day for the good of the company. To be resisted or rejected causes disappointment. That disappointment can be directed internally or at those with whom you are trying to work. Just like anger, evaluate what has caused your disappointment. Use it as motivation to find better ways to deliver on the transformation you are championing.

3. **Show Up.**
   A classic Zig Ziglar mantra is step three: "No matter how you feel . . . get up, dress us, show up and Never Give Up!" Take a pause if you need to in a moment of anger or disappointment. But, come back stronger and more determined. Your work is needed -- whether those you are trying to help realize it or not.

Learn your silo wall lessons. Use them to make you stronger. Then, you make the silos stronger.

Chapter 10

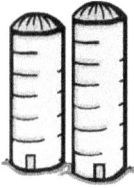

Everything is Process

"If you can't describe what you are doing as a process, you don't know what you are doing."

 - *W. Edwards Deming*

Think about when you wake up on a typical "work" morning. What do you do? Routines change little from morning to morning. Within that routine are tasks such as bathing, getting dressed, taking care of children, taking care of pets and perhaps doing some chores around the house to name a few.

While the activities vary from person to person, for any one person they are largely identical from day to day. The sense of routine applies to such detail as what shoe is put on first and brushing teeth before or after a shower. That routine is process. It is the series of steps followed to

Resource Snapshot

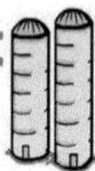

The Power of Habit
Charles Duhigg

The Power of Habit focuses on understanding how habits are formed and reformed. Duhigg explains the process of habit in a clear and understandable way. Using the core process of "cue-routine-reward," Duhigg breaks down habits and exposes how someone can change their own habits and influence the habits of others.

Key Quote
"The Golden Rule of Habit Change: You can't extinguish a bad habit, you can only change it."

Website
http://charlesduhigg.com/the-power-of-habit

Why this Resource?
Habit is simply another word for process. And process is at the core of all business activity. As a Hub Leader, having the skill to form and reform habits (process) is vital to success.

www.silostopillars.com/resource-snapshot

achieve a particular outcome. From getting ready for work to performing brain surgery, everything is driven by process.

The Unknown Process

Many struggle with the idea of process being everywhere and everything is process. The argument goes that process cannot be that universal because nobody keeps track of all those processes. So, is there really is a process if it is not identified? Yes, there is a process.

Many processes of daily life are virtually invisible. The routines followed when someone rises and goes to bed are good examples. They have been in place for so long they are unknown. To test this, make a conscious effort to do something different when going to bed and see how it feels. It will feel awkward and uncomfortable. Often it leads to forgetting to do something always previously done. This is because it is contrary to the process.

In his book, *The Power of Habit*, author Charles Duhigg describes it this way:

> When a habit emerges, the brain stops fully participating in the decision making. It stops working so hard, or diverts focus to other tasks. So, unless you deliberately fight a habit -- unless you find new routines -- the pattern will unfold automatically.

Process creates habit. Habit works automatically. People do not think about how they brush their teeth. They do not think about how they drive to work. They do not analyze how they button a shirt.

The same is true at work. Much of the routine work that is part of peoples' lives are habit. It is automatic. In fact, a well-designed process should be that automatic. It relieves the brain of paying attention based on the muscle memory of performing a task.

So, having an unknown process is not unusual. In fact, it should be common. It should be expected. The challenge is when one does not identify those sets of actions you take every day at home or at work as process. As a Hub Leader, those processes must be called out, assessed for effectiveness and replaced if change is needed. Remember, unknown process is still process.

The Ineffective Process

Some believe no process exists if something does not get accomplished accurately all the time. This misses the point. When a set of actions does not result in the right outcome, it does not demonstrate the lack of process. It demonstrates an ineffective process. Every ineffective process is both positive and negative.

The primary negative of an ineffective process is that it is, well, ineffective. It does not support the output expected and the customer's need is not satisfied. This does not have to be a permanent situation. As Winston Churchill said, "success is not final, failure is not fatal; it is the courage to continue that counts." This is where the positive side of an ineffective process begins.

If you know the process is ineffective, you are i) aware of the process and ii) that it is not producing what is expected. This puts you ahead of most. From there, you can fix the process if you choose. When the process is improved, it more accurately and consistently delivers. With every process improvement, your organization is better and your customers are better served.

The Hub Leader addresses ineffective processes through integrating Core Threads. If a process does not have quality, regulatory compliance or security (among others) designed into its execution, it is ineffective by definition.

> *[U]nknown process is still process.*

Without the Core Thread components embodied in the process, the customer is not getting what it needs. The Hub Leader uses this gap as one of the levers to more effectively work with Operations to transform the silo into a pillar.

Lasso Process to Propel

Process is the energy that drives execution in Operations. It is the catalyst for success. Some resist the discipline and structure of process arguing they are confining and stifling. Yet, structure and discipline are required for process to work. Without structure and discipline, process goes from propelling the business to being an unbridled explosion of energy that scatters delivery, damages the company and fails its customers.

In the movie *October Sky*, Homer Hickam, Jr. (played by Jake Gyllenhaal) is the son of a coal miner. Homer becomes fascinated with rockets and teams with three of his high school friends to build a rocket for a science fair. This allows them to learn rocket science and pursue their dream of being part of the U.S. effort to chase down the Russians who had recently launched the *Sputnik* rocket.

During his adventure, Homer learns that a rocket operates based on a simple principle of harnessing an explosion of energy and focusing it in a singular direction to achieve propulsion. That conversion of energy to propulsion is achieved through a simple device known as a throat identified in the basic rocket diagram below.

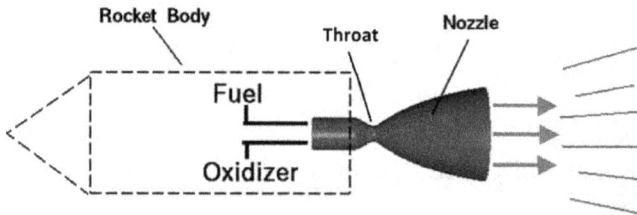

The throat is installed between the combustion chamber (the source of energy) and the nozzle (the rocket end that propels the rocket). The throat creates structure around the energy in the rocket and disciplines it to exit the rocket in a thrust of power to move the rocket the direction desired.

Successful businesses act in largely the same way as a rocket. There is a tremendous amount energy created by the talented team working within a company. This is the business' combustion chamber. Properly designed processes create the structure and discipline needed to harness the business' energy and focus it in the desired direction.

Process is to a business as the throat is to a rocket. Without it, both the business and rocket have energy, but the energy is an explosion without direction. The rocket components of a business are shown in the diagram below.

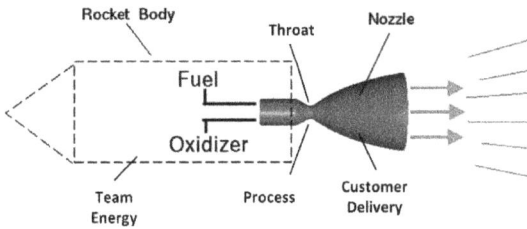

All business leaders need to be process leaders. Without structured, disciplined processes, the business cannot optimize its outcomes and suffers as a result. Hub Leaders must be particularly adept at process. They should focus on designing the Core Threads into Operations to optimize process which in turn propels the company to deliver on customer needs.

Chapter 11

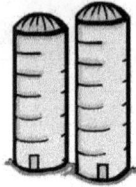

Dip Mentality

*"It's the little details that are vital. Little things make big
things happen."*

- John Wooden

Earlier we discussed Pour Mentality which is
characterized by the pouring of syrup over a stack of
pancakes. There is plenty of syrup poured. But, it is highly
ineffective and provides little to most of those for whom the
syrup is intended. The same is true of top down compliance
programs that pour content over operational silo leaders
and then are surprised that most (if not all) of the message
never makes it to the front line.

Staying with our pancake example from before, syrup
distribution is vastly improved with Dip Mentality.

Resource Snapshot

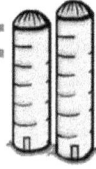

Lovability
Brian DeHaaff

Lovability is a journey into a whole new world of business innovation, growth and success. DeHaaff, using the values and business acumen of his grandparents, developed a "human-centered approach" to starting Aha!, his SaaS software platform. *Lovability* exposes the values that support Aha!'s continued growth and employee engagement.

Key Quote

"We wanted to do something different, something true . . . . We also wanted to create a place where people would love to work. We were tired of investors who put greed before dignity and human well-being."

Website

www.aha.io/lovability

Why this Resource?

Hub Leaders should treat the transformation of silos to pillars as their personal start up. DeHaaff charts a course to make the Hub Leader's work meaningful for customers, valuable for the organization and fun for those executing the work.

www.silostopillars.com/resource-snapshot

Dip Mentality is focused on delivery of Compliance throughout the silo from leadership to the frontline staff. Rather than pouring the syrup over the top, Dip Mentality addresses each element of the silo. It identifies the pieces within the silo and delivers the Core Threads to them as needed.

Focus on the Pieces

John Wooden was the legendary basketball coach of the UCLA Bruins from 1948 through 1975. Known as the "Wizard of Westwood," Wooden's Bruins won 10 NCAA men's basketball championships, including a record seven in a row. Yet, in the midst of such rampant success, it was Wooden's attention to detail that set him apart.

Wooden was well-known for his first day of practice "socks and shoes" lessons. Each season, he would first teach his players the critical basketball skill of *putting on their socks and shoes!* Players such as Lew Alcindor (later known as Kareem Abdul-Jabbar) and Bill Walton were shocked at the painstaking detail with which Coach Wooden would teach the lessons.

Some might think that the socks and shoes lessons were a tactic by which the wily coach would humble his newly recruited players. Demanding perfection on something as trivial as putting on shoes and socks might help Wooden gain control of the players who envisioned great success for themselves.

The lessons, however, were not a tactic. In 2008, Coach Wooden taught the lessons to a young cancer patient at a charity event and explained the lessons were part of being able to play basketball at a high level. As Wooden put it:

> *You know, basketball is a game that's played on a hardwood floor. And to be good, you have to ... change your direction, change your pace. That's hard on your feet. Your feet are very important. And if you don't have every wrinkle out of your sock, you'll get blisters.*

Dip Mentality takes the same painstaking approach to ensuring each piece of every silo gets what it needs when it comes to the Core Threads syrup. If there is a failure to get the needed syrup to every piece of the silo, a whole host of

> *[Dip Mentality] identifies the pieces within the silo and delivers the Core Threads to them as needed.*

negative outcomes occur. These negative outcomes in your business are no different than Coach Wooden's players getting "blisters."

Think Pull

Dip Mentality is not nearly as simple as Pour Mentality. It is much easier to simply pour the Core Threads over Operations and hope it sticks. The ease of Pour Mentality is a crutch for many leaders. They default to the less effective method of simply pouring information over the top of teams. With Pour Mentality, the leader **pushes** information, strategy and education on people and hopes it works.

Dip Mentality is more difficult. It relies on a **pull** system in which all silo members take the strategy, information and education as needed. Affording people the opportunity to pull Core Thread information on demand requires the leader to i) know the Core Threads "syrup"; ii) know the silo staff's work and ii) understand the relevance and application of the Core Threads to the silo staff to know when and how they will need the syrup.

The increased effort of Dip Mentality is due to the need for more careful delivery. Both Pour and Dip Mentality require the leader be knowledgeable about the Core Threads being woven into the silo's fabric. Pour dumps syrup over operations' head when the Pour leader wants to pour.

Dip Mentality understands the silo is dynamic and that all the syrup must be available when it is needed within the silo. Leaders with Dip Mentality understand the silo's workings and its members' needs. From there, a comprehensive system emerges to adapt to those silo workings and members' needs.

Dip Means All Get the Syrup

Remember what happened to the syrup that was poured? It landed on the top pancake and simply ran down the sides of the stack leaving most of the pancakes dry. Dip Mentality leaves no one without the syrup.

The Hub Leader uses Dip Mentality and cuts into the stack of pancakes to access all. The Hub Leader gets to know the siloed Operations leader as well as the Operations team at all levels. The Hub Leader understands deeply the nature of Operations' culture. The Hub Leader envisions and plans where to intervene as a value- added partner. The Hub Leader works to get all what they need.

Only through this detailed approach does true Core Thread integration take place. Weaving the Core Threads blossoms at the front line. All get the syrup because the Hub Leader knows this is the only way to ensure success.

Chapter 12

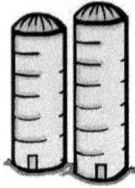

Weave Core Threads into Operations

"We sleep, but the loom of life never stops, and the pattern which was weaving when the sun went down is weaving when it comes up in the morning."

- Henry Ward Beecher

The Wind and the Sun were disputing which was the stronger. Suddenly they saw a traveler coming down the road, and the Sun said: "I see a way to decide our dispute. Whichever of us can cause that traveler to take off his cloak shall be regarded as the stronger. You begin." So the Sun retired behind a cloud, and the Wind began to blow as hard as it could upon the traveler. But the harder he blew the more closely did the traveler wrap his cloak round him, till at last the Wind had to give up in despair. Then the Sun came out and shone in all his glory upon the traveler, who soon found it too hot to walk with his cloak on.

Aesop's Fables

Resource Snapshot

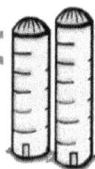

The Energy Bus
Jon Gordon

The Energy Bus is a parable about how to build a team and position its members for optimal performance. Gordon tells the story of George, a business leader with a home life in disarray and a work team not much better. *The Energy Bus* follows George's journey to learn the 10 rules "for the ride of his life."

Key Quote
"You're the Driver of Your Bus."

Website
www.theenergybus.com

Why this Resource?
Being a Hub Leader can be hard. In fact, it is often hard. It can be hard on the Hub Leader personally and it can be hard on the team helping the Hub Leader. Energy is a primary antidote when challenges come. *The Energy Bus* can help with that antidote.

www.silostopillars.com/resource-snapshot

When you begin to take the responsibility to weave the Core Threads into your business, remember the Sun. Recognize that what allows you to weave is your willingness to give. The reason the Sun was able to cause the traveler to remove his cloak was because the Sun gave warmth. The warmth made the cloak unnecessary.

The Hub Leader takes the same approach. What is it that you can give to ease the stress of your operational colleagues? What are their pain points? What keeps them up at night? Those sound like sales questions. They are. Hub Leaders understand that they deliver results to the customer by delivering service to Operations. So, Hub Leaders focus on solving Operations' pain points; this facilitates Operations doing the same for the customer.

Operations Drives the Bus

When Hub Leaders take on the task of weaving Core Threads, they focus all effort through Operations. Again, Operations is your business' breadwinner. Without Operations, there is no business to support. To be effective, Hub Leaders must remember Operations' primary role in the business and defer to it as the Hub Leader works.

So what does this Hub Leader deference mean? It means that Hub Leaders adapt their work to Operations. Core Threads are adapted to the business to become intuitive elements of operational processes. Operations does not adapt to the Core Threads.

This relationship between Core Threads and Operations makes sense. A perfectly designed quality program is of little good to an operation that is not successful. A bankrupt business does not need a strong business continuity plan.

Core Threads are designed and deployed in a manner to strengthen Operations. Core Threads focus on outcomes. The Hub Leader understands these outcomes can be achieved in a number of ways. Success happens when the Hub Leader executes the Core Threads in a manner that strengthens and improves Operations' success.

Core Threads Keep Operations on the Road

Operations driving the bus does not diminish the value of the Core Threads. The Hub Leader understands the need for the Core Threads to create the ongoing, sustainable success of the company through delivery that meets customer needs.

There are a number of Core Threads. Which apply to particular industries varies. Here is a brief summary of five common Core Threads:

- **Compliance**

  Compliance has seen a dramatic increase in focus across a wide variety of industries. From U.S. Federal healthcare compliance requirements to Foreign Corrupt Practices Act, Financial Industry Regulatory Authority to the National Highway Safety Traffic Administration, the web of agencies and regulators continues to drive increased requirements for businesses. Compliance is a critical design component of process to ensure meeting the growing requirements placed on businesses. Failure to comply often result in fines and other sanctions that no business needs.

- **Continuity**

  Customers engage your company because of risk (solve a problem/capture an opportunity). In doing so, the customer is trusting part of its delivery to your company. Continuity is the program that plans for and ensures your business is resilient to the events that may interrupt your ability to deliver. Items such as business impact analysis, disaster recovery of IT systems, alternate work locations and work around procedures are key to an effective continuity program. Continuity is a key process design component because it creates the ability for the company to resist interruption events and respond effectively to resume operations when interruptions actually occur.

- **Quality**

  Quality is the program that ensures i) what the company delivers is accurate based on product/service specifications and ii) the company delivers what the customer requested. Items such as internal audit, supplier management, nonconforming events and continual improvement are central to quality programs. Quality is a key process design component because it ensures the appropriate monitors and controls are in place so the customer receives what is ordered within specification.

- **Safety**

  Safety serves two purposes within a company. First, safety can apply to the safety of the products and services the company produces. Second, safety can apply to the safety of workers who are employed by the company. Items such as ergonomics, hazard communication and safe energy practices are important to the effective safety program. Safety is a key design component within your company because it protects your workers and the consumers of your product/services.

- **Security**
  Data is a continually increasing risk for businesses
  around the globe. As more systems interconnect
  globally across the Internet, the security and privacy of
  data becomes of greater importance to businesses and
  individuals. Breaches of data from private and
  governmental entities around the world demonstrate
  the need for robust data security. Items such as
  vulnerability management, data loss prevention, asset
  hardening and patching are vital to an effective
  security program. Security is a key design element for
  processes because it strengthens the data protection
  that companies, regulators and individuals require.

No matter which Core Threads apply to your
particular business, they are important to strengthen your
processes. Weaving the Core Threads into your processes is
the place where "layering" transforms into "integrating"
and your silos become pillars.

Solve Within the Operations Mindset

Operations mindset is how operational leaders look
at the business -- producing products or services for
customers. Knowing this, how does the Hub Leader use the
operations mindset to solve the Core Thread challenges
facing the business?

The Hub Leader approaches integrating the Core
Threads consistent with how an Operations leader
approaches Operations – it is all part of producing products
and services for customers. There is no other calling and
no other objective than to serve the customer. Customer
delivery is done through a single, integrated workflow that
begins with the customer's needs and ends with the
company's satisfaction of those customer needs.

The operations mindset sees the work through this singular workflow. The Hub Leader solves problems in the operations mindset by working within that same singular workflow. There is no stand-alone compliance, quality or security program. There is no us versus them. There is no we and they. There is only <u>us</u> and together we serve the customer.

The Delancey Street Foundation is an excellent example of this approach. Delancey Street was founded in San Francisco in 1971 with 4 people and a $1,000.00 loan. Its vision, then and now, is "to turn around the lives of people in poverty, substance abusers, former felons, and

> *Core Threads are adapted to the business to become intuitive elements of operational processes. Operations does not adapt to the Core Threads.*

others who have hit bottom, *by empowering the people with the problems to become the solution.*"

Today, Delancey Street Foundation oversees more than a dozen programs in cities throughout the United States and is regarded as one of the country's most successful rehabilitation programs.

Delancey Street Foundation has a number of unique qualities that have created its success. One of the more remarkable attributes of Delancey Street Foundation programs is that they are all centered on business operations (e.g., food service, trucking, digital printing, etc.). It is from these business organizations that Delancey Street Foundation delivers rehabilitation opportunities to a wide range of people "who have hit rock bottom."

How do they do this? Delancey Street Foundation weaves its rehabilitation activities into operations. People who come to a Delancey Street program immediately have a job within an organization. They have tasks to perform. They do those tasks under the supervision of someone who may have had the same job just a few days before. That supervisor also has similar life challenges as well.

Through this similarity of experience, a person's rehabilitative needs begin to be met as a natural part of the business' operations. Delancey Street Foundation has rehabilitated thousands of people through this operations mindset.

The Hub Leader can do the same thing with the Core Threads. When the Hub Leader commits to the operations mindset, progress happens in a much different way. Rather than trying to plan how Operations can adopt each Core Thread, the focus shifts to how each Core Thread works in Operations.

Integration and intuitive design become the hallmarks of the Hub Leader's work. Just like Delancey Street Foundation, staff members are no longer taught Core Threads through awareness programs. Staff members are fully aware of the Core Threads because they become part and parcel of how the staff performs work.

The Process Profile

The operations mindset is how the Hub Leader transforms silos into pillars. The Process Profile is one of the Hub Leader's primary tools. The Process Profile becomes the gateway through which the Hub Leader designs the Core Threads into operational process and engages in the collaborative work that creates pillars.

The Process Profile is not prescriptive. It is a flexible tool for the Hub Leader. The Process Profile is the tool with which a Hub Leader captures and manages three key process data point types: design, optimize and comply.

- **Design**

  Design data points focus on a business' process command and control. Hub Leaders capture detailed process flows of the steps within each process as well as the tools used in each step.

  The design data captures process failure points so risk can be assessed and treated. While it may not be possible to eliminate all failure points, the design data educates the Hub Leader and the Operations where things could go wrong. When the failure points are known, monitors and controls are designed into the process steps to ensure the process works properly.

  The design data also addresses the effective design of workflows (multiple integrated processes). Design data exposes the inputs to all processes, the work done within the process and the output to other processes or the customer. With this information, the Operations leader has insight into how work is accomplished from customer order to delivery. The Hub Leader sees where the Core Threads need to be integrated to strengthen the workflow.

- **Optimize**

  Optimize data supports the Hub Leader working collaboratively with Operations to identify the performance characteristics of each process. What is the required or expected throughput? How much work can each staff member produce within each discrete step of the process?

  The optimize data drives process management. It gives the Operations leader an insight tool to oversee processes either in real time or on a prescribed cadence. It supports reporting performance metrics to employees to create a visual workplace so they can monitor their performance individually and as a team. Optimize data lets Operations know if things are going as planned or if something has gone askew.

The optimize data exposes the process' performance for the Operations leader to understand the path of production. Operations can see bottlenecks or other throughput constraints that negatively impact delivery. The optimize data presents the Operations leader with the big picture through the little pictures painted within each discrete process. The optimize data gives visibility to identify when improvement or rework is needed within a workflow or process.

- **Comply**
  Comply data identifies the risks and solutions the Core Threads address. It ties the Core Thread requirements directly to the process steps Operations executes.

  For example, rather than having a safety program discussing the need for personal protective equipment (PPE) such as gloves, hard hats, etc., the comply data embeds the PPE requirement into the Process Profile at the applicable process steps the employee performs. This transforms the safety program from something layered on from the outside to an integrated part of the work designed into what staff does every day.

  It is much easier for staff to create a habit (read process) of compliance when they understand not only what the requirement is, but also where and how it fits into their daily work. Rather than having a compliance professional telling them in an awareness meeting to handle things in a particular way, comply data educates Operations on the compliance requirement as an intuitive part of the work. This creates buy-in because it is part of the process (think habit) of Operations.

The comply data encompasses all the necessary Core Threads for the business. From what sort of data is being handled (Security) to what do I do if there is an interruption to this process (Continuity), the comply data becomes a beacon to Operations staff and leadership on what to do with those non-operational elements of process.

Later, in Part 5, we discuss how to weave the Core Threads into operational processes. You use the data from the Process Profile as the raw material for your design. This transforms silos into pillars. Before that, it is important to understand the Hub Leader, who is the master weaver.

Part 4

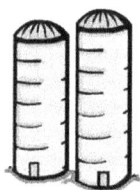

The Hub Leader

Part 2

Chapter 13

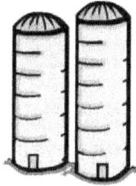

Be _the_ Hub, Not _a_ Spoke

"The mind is like a richly woven tapestry in which the colors are distilled from the experiences of the senses, and the designs drawn from the convolutions of the intellect."

- _Carson McCullers_

It takes a special kind of leader to execute the transition of silos into pillars. It takes a Hub Leader. Someone who is willing and able to navigate the ever-changing environment of the siloed and sometimes matrixed organization. Up to now we have identified the Hub Leader as one who champions the silo-to-pillar transition. Here, we look at what makes up the Hub Leader.

Before we dive into the Hub Leader, it is important to understand Hub Leadership is an approach to leadership. It relies on foundational leadership skills taught

Resource Snapshot

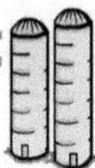

Linchpin
Seth Godin

Linchpin takes readers through a journey to their best, most indispensable self. Godin contrasts the commodity business model with its obedient workers with the indispensable company, with its linchpin team. He contrasts it at both the organization and personal level to emphasize the need to be remarkable at both.

Key Quote

"Those are the only two choices. Win by being more ordinary, more standard, and cheaper. Or win by being faster, more remarkable, and more human."

Website

www.sethgodin.com

Why this Resource?

Transforming silos to pillars requires a divergence from the commodity. When a pillar is created, your business becomes remarkable. *Linchpin* guides you to that place personally and organizationally.

www.silostopillars.com/resource-snapshot

by renowned experts such as John Maxwell, Barbara Corcoran, Tom Peters and Simon Sinek, to name a few. If these skills do not exist, then the approach does not work.

Hub Leadership focuses on transforming silos into the pillars to drive sustainable success for your company. Below are key attributes of the Hub Leader's performance. The points below may seem simple.

Do not take the simplicity as an indication of ease. Being a Hub Leader is hard. What it offers in simplicity, it takes back in its challenge. But the rewards for your business and your career are immeasurable.

The image below visually represents the Hub Leader and shows how the Hub Leader is positioned related to the customer and the business:

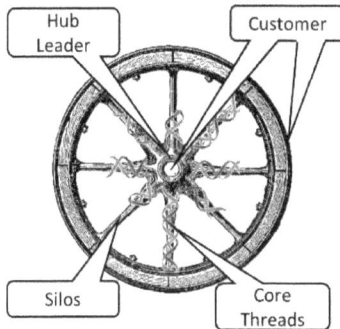

As with all things in the organization, the customer is at the center. The customer is also on the edge of the wheel where "the rubber meets the road." The Hub Leader is represented, not surprisingly, by the hub of the wheel that encircles the customer.

The spokes of the wheel represent the operational silos in the organization. The ribbons wrapped around each spoke at various levels represent the Core Threads. The length the ribbons are wrapped around each spoke indicates how deeply the Core Threads have been woven into that particular silo.

The Hub Leader's objective is to weave the Core Threads across all the silos and down the spokes to ultimately reach the customer at the outside of the wheel. With each progressive step weaving down the spoke, the silo is strengthened to deliver to the customer. When fully woven, the silo becomes a pillar that supports the business.

The Hub Connects

The first Hub Leader focus is connection. This is how a hub works on a wheel. It holds the spokes together at the center of the wheel to give it strength and balance. The same is true for the Hub Leader.

In the picture above, the Core Threads are woven to different lengths on each spoke. Weaving the Core Threads is not uniform across all silos. Each silo represents a unique challenge to the Hub Leader for a variety of reasons. Thus, the Hub Leader's work connects the Core Threads within silos and connects the Core Threads' messages across silos to create consistency and drive adoption.

To achieve connection, the Hub Leader is keenly aware of the needs and requirements within all business areas. Hub Leaders cannot be successful sitting in their offices. They need to be out with business leaders gaining insight into how various silos work, what various silos need and how best to create connection. From there, the Hub Leader connects with and across silos.

Do Not Be Partisan

Hub Leaders are human. As a connector across the organization, the Hub Leader encounters a wide variety of people and groups. They naturally prefer working with certain people or groups more than others. Despite this, Hub Leaders step out of their comfort zone to engage with all these disparate operational leaders across the organization.

A key metric to ensure non-partisanship is the time the Hub Leader spends in each area of the business. A good Hub Leader can i) spend equal time

> *The Hub Leader's objective is to weave the Core Threads across all the silos, down the spokes and ultimately to the customer at the outside of the wheel.*

with all groups or ii) spend greater time with groups who most need what the Hub Leader has to offer. Equal time is easier to administer. A more risk/need-based approach is more effective.

The Hub Leader continually evaluates the people and groups with whom the Hub Leader works. Those that need more help or present the greatest risk to the organization get the most time. This is a Hub Leadership challenge. The leaders who are not receptive (and possibly hostile) to the Hub Leader's work are the people with whom the Hub Leader needs to spend more time. These reluctant leaders can be a drain on the Hub Leader.

Yet, despite this challenge, it is these very leaders with whom the Hub Leader can have the most positive impact. Thus, more time is required.

The uneven distribution of time does not undermine the effort to connect all areas. Those groups needing less time still need the right time from the Hub Leader. It is a delicate balance and one that delivers on the effort expended.

Cross-Pollinate the Best

The Hub Leader first achieves connection. Then, the Hub Leader engages silos in the manner and by the means needed by each to optimize the Core Threads. From these two actions, the Hub Leader cross pollinates the best of the organization.

Earlier we discussed evaluating silos and how they interact. One thing to evaluate was how and for what silos are sought out by other silos. The Hub Leader is in a unique position to drive that analysis even deeper.

The Hub Leader sees from an objective first-hand perspective the silo's operational processes as well as the silo's strengths and weaknesses. It is this unique vantage point that is so valuable. The Hub Leader has no allegiance except to the company. So, the Hub Leader can be dispassionate. Things are seen for what they are -- good and bad.

Seeing the good and bad creates clarity on what should and should not be promoted throughout the organization. Knowing what not to do is as valuable as knowing what to do. Philosopher John Stuart Mill, in his work *On Liberty* makes the same argument related to the exchange of ideas -- good or bad, true or false.

Mill believed the exchange of ideas causes people to reexamine and reaffirm their beliefs. The same is true of the Hub Leader. By seeing and evaluating the good and the bad, the Hub Leader is a key contributor to the organization's continual improvement.

Cross pollinating best practices across the organization is a key value of the Hub Leader. Rather than simply carrying a bag full of requirements throughout the company's silos, the Hub Leader is a consultant of excellence by highlighting the things that work (and do not work) to leaders throughout the company.

The Hub Leader can encourage and arm operational leaders with strategies and tactics that have been successful elsewhere in the company and warn those same leaders of things that have not worked.

The Hub Leader elevates the entire organization. The best of the company is embedded throughout the company. Great ideas and approaches can be replicated. Mistakes can be avoided. Because the Hub Leader has no allegiance to anything except the company, the ideas can be disseminated without any competitive angst or bias. The ideas are offered for the company's good, period.

But, When the Bad Thing Happens . . .

The Hub Leader is not an identified position within an organization. It is an approach to leadership within the organization. The Hub Leader holds an important oversight role (compliance officer, quality manager, security director, etc.). From that position within the organization, they take on the Hub Leader approach to enhance the value they can bring to the organization. Yet, while they are working toward being their best Hub Leader, they are still executing their oversight role.

This distinction between the Hub Leader approach you take and the title you hold is vitally important when the day comes that the "Bad Thing" happens. What is the Bad Thing? Simply stated, the Bad Thing is an event which occurs in every organization when actions occur which are inconsistent with the organization's requirements. It is a variance from a regulatory requirement. It is a quality failure in Operations. It is a data breach of numerous sensitive records. It is a Code of Conduct violation.

The Bad Thing demands that you step both feet into your oversight role. This is not the moment of integration and understanding the value of the silo. This is when you are called upon to stand in the gap, protect the organization and do what customers need you to do.

We do not, however, have to set aside all we know (and will know) about the Hub Leader approach. In fact, Hub Leader skills make you more effective in addressing the Bad Thing with Operations, your organization and your customers. Here are just a few of the Hub Leader traits that shine in the face of the Bad Thing:

- **Know the Facts**
  It is easy to jump to conclusions. Conclusions without all the facts can be deadly when dealing with the Bad Thing. The only and ultimate goal is to reach the correct conclusion based on the facts. Talk to whomever you need to ensure you know the facts. If you have a question, ask it. If something does not make sense, keep asking questions until it does. Your actions from a base of facts are what is needed.

- **Work Exclusively From the Facts**
  Emotions are the enemy of a thorough investigation and response to the Bad Thing. Emotions take facts and twist them to fit a particular narrative. Some call it spin. No matter what one calls it, doing anything to alter or filter facts ultimately leaves you with something other than the facts. That presents a very real risk of making a decision that is misaligned with what really happened.

- **Avoid Measuring Intent**
  One of the traps when responding to the Bad Thing is to attempt to assess intent. "Why did they do this?" is a dangerous path to take during the Bad Thing. There is little value in trying to uncover why someone did something. The pursuit of facts should not be clouded by the issue of intent. Intent is a matter of the mind and heart. For most, these are arenas beyond their competency. Stick to the facts.

- **Advocate for Clarity**
  Do not shortcut the review of the Bad Thing. Seek a full understanding of the facts. Advocate to leadership that taking a bit more time to achieve clarity of the facts brings great value to the organization because the review will be

credible. Any increase in speed to conclusion is far outweighed by achieving clarity.

- **<u>Maintain Standards Without Piety</u>**

  When you ultimately achieve clarity about the facts and have identified the actors involved in those facts, you are then in a position to report those facts to others for action. It is tempting to add your personal "flavor" to the report and talk about how terrible this Bad Thing is. You may want to go further and comment on those involved. Avoid that temptation. You may feel justified because of previous resistance to your work from the organization or those involved in the Bad Thing. Your piety to settle the score and be seen as more valuable to the organization will not work. It casts you as a martyr. Martyrs make for good drama. They do not make for good organizational leaders.

Chapter 14

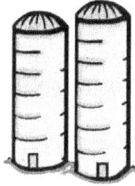

Soften the Ground

"Whosoever desires constant success must change his conduct with the times."

- Niccolo Machiavelli

A Hub Leader is like a farmer -- sowing seeds and reaping harvests. A farmer has the courage to envision a greater tomorrow and the faith to pursue that vision. The ground is the primary tool for every farmer to produce crops or grow livestock. Many a country song has been written about the farmer working the land to provide for community and family.

The Hub Leader has the same sort of ground. It is not necessarily a plot of soil. It is the organization the Hub Leader is privileged to serve. The ground is the collective culture that makes up the organization and the people in

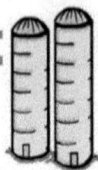

Resource Snapshot
Yes, And
Kelly Leonard and Tom Yorton

Yes, And is a product of The Second City improvisational theater company. Leonard and Yorton begin with the premise that business is one great improvisation. From there, they take the reader through an Improvisation 101 primer that pays immediate dividends. A reader can take away an entirely new set of skills and techniques to communicate more effectively for problem solving or any other business purpose.

Key Quote
"No matter what title is on your business card, professional success requires the ability to create something out of nothing, which is in many ways at the heart of what it means to improvise."

Website
www.secondcity.com

Why this Resource?
Becoming a Hub Leader, weaving Core Threads and transforming silos into pillars likely has no precedent in your company. You are truly creating something from nothing. *Yes, And* can help.

www.silostopillars.com/resource-snapshot

it. And just like the soil with which the farmer works, the ground the Hub Leader encounters has both fertile areas and rocky patches. How the Hub Leader softens all the ground, fertile and rocky, determines the Hub Leader's success.

Operations is Not Waiting on You

The Hub Leader will wait a considerable time before an engraved invitation from Operations arrives. There is no reason to believe Operations wants your help, will seek your help or is waiting for your help. To the contrary, Operations has its own work to do and the Hub Leader is not on the agenda.

This lack of invitation is not a negative. As we talked about earlier, silos resist outsiders. That is why the outside of the silo wall exists. The silo views the Hub Leader as a distraction to its work. Worse yet, Hub Leaders are not operations people. So, they have the double negative of being an uninformed distraction.

As for the lack of invitation from Operations, it actually can work to the Hub Leader's advantage. It lets the Hub Leader choose the rules of engagement. The Hub Leader gets to identify the strategy to follow, the timing to connect and the goals to pursue before ever entering an Operations silo. Take advantage of this space as it presents the runway to establishing the critical relationships which supports the Hub Leader's success.

Become a Trusted Advisor

While Hub Leaders do not typically bring customers, revenue or execution on the delivery of products or services, they bring a vision, expertise and perspective that Operations does not have, but needs. While that expertise, vision and perspective are important, their value must be proven to Operations.

Recognizing what they do (and do not) bring to the table, Hub Leaders focus on becoming a trusted advisor. Upon earning the position of a trusted advisor, the Hub Leader builds a

> *And just like the soil with which the farmer works, the ground the Hub Leader encounters has both fertile areas and rocky patches.*

sustainable relationship with Operations that delivers value to the silo which ultimately delivers value to the organization.

What does that trusted advisor relationship look like? At its core, the trusted advisor relationship is characterized by i) open dialogue; ii) real consideration (although not always agreement) of the Hub Leader's input and iii) access to the Operations leader's world. When the Hub Leader achieves these three elements on a consistent basis, a trusted advisor relationship exists.

Credibility

To become a trusted advisor, the Hub Leader must establish and maintain credibility. In the relationship with Operations, it is almost certain the Hub Leader does not bring superior operational expertise to relationship. In fact, the Hub Leader is not there to augment Operations' expertise.

Rather, the Hub Leader is contributing Core Threads expertise which is largely non-operational and intangible. The Core Threads are intangible because they focus more on prevention than repair. Core Threads prevent bad things from happening. They ensure Operations' delivery is sound. It is hard to measure what does not happen.

Because Hub Leaders trade in things that are largely intangible, credibility is their currency. When they prove themselves credible and trustworthy, Operations continues to explore and deepen the relationship. When they act in ways that are not credible and lack candor, doors close.

Once the Hub Leader acknowledges the indispensable need for credibility, the follow up question is "what does that mean to the work I do?" The answer is the Hub Leader's credibility is protected at all costs.

Honesty and transparency are at the top of the Hub Leader's list. When there is a choice between the Hub Leader's credibility versus anything, credibility wins. Speed loses. Perceived wins lose. Everything loses. Because, without credibility, the Hub Leader's work is done.

Help Create Readiness

In tying this together, consider one last question. If the goal is to become a trusted advisor through maintaining credibility with Operations, what is the Hub Leader trying to achieve? In short, readiness.

The Core Threads are things that regulators, accreditors and customers expect from organizations. They prevent bad things from happening in Operations. The Core

Threads may be non-operational in nature, but they are executed within Operations. Thus, the strongest outcome for the Hub Leader is to create a state of readiness for Operations to demonstrate the Core Threads within its processes.

Readiness is achieved through weaving the Core Threads into operational process. This means the Core Threads occur because operational processes are running. The Hub Leader is the ultimate weaver for the benefit of the customer, the organization and the operational silo. Readiness is not for the sake of the Hub Leader or the Core Threads.

Readiness is for the company and its customers. This allows the Hub Leader to serve Operations and adapt the Core Threads to Operations. This becomes the path to readiness.

Chapter 15

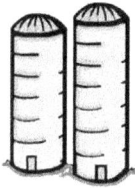

Be an Advocate, Not an Expert

"Advocacy is a communicative act. Advocacy is also a persuasive act. Advocacy not only means endorsing a cause or idea, but recommending, promoting, defending, or arguing for it."

— *John Capecci and Timothy Cage, <u>Living Proof</u>*

In the Introduction, we talked about lawyers. Here, we discuss a primary tool with which lawyers (and Hub Leaders) practice their craft -- advocacy. Hub Leaders have a passion for what they are doing as they navigate through and among the silos of an organization. Their only allegiance and objective is to make the company better so it can better serve its customers. Deviation from that primary mission diminishes the Hub Leader's success.

The Core Threads can stretch the Hub Leader's expertise. Is it possible for a Hub Leader to be an expert in risk management, quality, information security,

Resource Snapshot

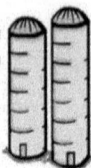

Re-imagine!
Tom Peters

Re-imagine! Is a manifesto about the evolution of work in the 21st century. Peters, the author of *In Search of Excellence*, pens a unique, disruptive resource with *Re-imagine!*. He forces the reader to see the world as it is and will be rather than as a mere continuation of what has been.

Key Quote
"The 'value added' for most any company, tiny or enormous, comes from the . . . Quality of Experience provided."

Website
www.tompeters.com

Why this Resource?
Re-Imagine! gives the Hub Leader the means to make a significant difference in the business through making a difference for the customer. This resource motivates its readers to be different and be great.

www.silostopillars.com/resource-snapshot

compliance and business continuity (just to name a few of the Core Threads)? Likely not. Subject matter experts in all these areas exist who have devoted years to developing the skills and deep understanding of these subject areas. The Hub Leader collaborates with these experts.

So, how does the Hub Leader succeed with the Core Threads without being an expert? Advocacy.

The Hub Leader's role is part evangelist and part advocate for each of the Core Threads. No one needs to be an expert at physics to advocate the necessity and importance of using a parachute when skydiving.

The Hub Leader builds an environment in which the Core Threads can grow and flourish. Subject matter experts in all Core Thread areas are engaged and integrate within the environment the Hub Leader has fostered. Systems to integrate Core Threads into Operations are designed and implemented. In short, the Hub Leader builds the onramp to integrate them.

The Hub Leader does not necessarily have all the substantive Core Thread answers or expertise. Rather, the Hub Leader knows the Core Threads' importance and takes on the mission to inform, persuade and advocate for the Core Threads throughout the organization.

Work in the Macro

The Hub Leader's scope is broader than most. It encompasses many disparate areas. The Hub Leader works in the macro which means remaining focused on the company's overall operational system.

The Hub Leader resists the desire to focus in the weeds and become overwhelmed by the details. There are subject matter experts who work with the Hub Leader who can address these details. It is the Hub Leader's charge to ensure all work, even the work in the weeds, is framed in the context of the entire operational system.

The Hub Leader's system thinking ensures that the Core Threads are designed, implemented and executed consistent with each other and in concert with Operations. The Core Threads naturally fit into the overall Operations process. Working in the macro drives integration and avoids layering.

Help Experts Work in the Macro

Not only does the Hub Leader need to work in the macro, the Hub Leader needs to help Operations focus on the macro as well. As the relationship matures between the Hub Leader and Operations, a value the Hub Leader brings is a systems/macro level focus to the Core Threads design work.

Operations leaders are masters of detail. It is what supports their daily execution. Focus on the micro can have the same negative effect for the Operations leader as it does for the Hub Leader. It can create blinders. It can shift focus in directions that deter success. Just like the Hub Leader, the Operations leader has people on the team to address the micro details.

The Hub Leader is a catalyst for macro-level thinking. While the Core Threads work is not the Operations leader's primary focus, the Hub Leader helps evolve the Operations' leader through systems-level Core Thread design. This expands the Operations leader's perspective to not only improve the integration of Core Threads,

> *The Hub Leader's role is to be part evangelist and part advocate for each of the Core Threads.*

but also improve systems-level execution with Operations.

When the Operations leader understands that operational activities integrate into a system with Core Threads, there is greater clarity about how the Core Threads support daily execution. This clarity makes the Operations leader stronger and more open to sustainable dialogue and execution with the Hub Leader.

Help Operators Appreciate the Core Threads

This is Hub Leadership - Plus. The great Hub Leader is passionate about the Core Threads and respectful about the importance of Operations. That combination of passion and respect can present the opportunity to develop the Operations leader's appreciation of the Core Threads.

Two things to remember here: First, the Hub Leader's passion for the Core Threads must be coupled with a genuine appreciation for Operations. If there is any lack of respect for the challenges facing Operations, there is no chance to achieve Hub Leadership - Plus. If appreciation and respect exist, then the Hub Leader has the chance to help the Operations leader appreciate what the Hub Leader does to design the Core Threads into Operations' process and how it helps Operations deliver.

Second, the Hub Leader's passion and respect must be consistent. This does not mean the Hub Leader and Operations leader cannot disagree or have serious conversations about what is best for the company and its customers.

It does mean that the Hub Leader cannot lose focus on Operations as the company breadwinner and that the Core Threads exist to enhance Operations; they never take the primary seat ahead of Operations. If the Hub Leader makes this mistake, it is a long way back.

In the end, advocacy paves the road to weaving the Core Threads. It is the skill the Hub Leader taps more than any other.

Part 5

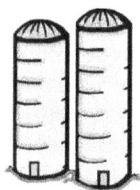

How to Weave

Chapter 16

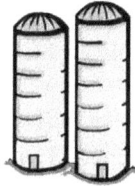

Assess the Environment

"Look before your leap"

-Ancient Proverb

We have talked about the value silos bring to an organization. We have looked at how non-operational players such as compliance, quality and continuity typically layer on additional requirements to Operations making its work more difficult.

We have explored how more effectively integrated work through Operations transforms silos into pillars and how a Hub Leader can create that transformation.

When you are at the threshold of actually transforming silos into pillars, you are contemplating a big step -- for you and your organization. The transformation requires an "all in" commitment. There is no half way or dipping your toe in the water. You are out on a branch

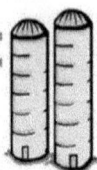

Resource Snapshot

The Advantage
Patrick Lencioni

In *The Advantage*, Patrick Lencioni identifies how to build, restore and sustain the health of an organization. Lencioni takes dead aim at the idea of "Organizational Health" and provides guidance to leaders about how to achieve this critical element of their businesses.

Key Quote
"The healthier an organization is, the more of its intelligence it is able to tap into and use."

Website
www.tablegroup.com

Why this Resource?
The Hub Leader creates tremendous change within an organization. As change progresses, strain is placed on the organization's health. *The Advantage* is a resource that sensitizes the Hub Leader to the importance of maintaining and improving Organizational Health as the transformation proceeds.

www.silostopillars.com/resource-snapshot

doing something special for your customers and company. You need to be sure the branch is strong. You also need to ensure there is not someone behind you with a saw.

You need to assess your company's capabilities and appetite for the change you are advocating.

More than Tone

First, you need to assess whether your organization's leaders are ready for the silo transformation. You need to understand if various executive and operational leaders support (or will support) the work of discussing, planning and executing silo transformation. You need to have conversations with these leaders to understand their mindset. Are they "comfortable"? How do they approach change? Are they motivated to make the company better for the sake of its customers?

You cannot simply ask these questions and take the answer at face value. The answer is always positive because leaders are universally committed to the right "tone at the top." Everyone embraces change until change is required. Everyone wants to get better until you ask them to do something different.

You need more than tone. Like the old saying goes, "what you do speaks so loudly, I cannot hear what you say." You must go beyond the talk. You must observe behavior and then discuss that behavior with key leaders. Why did they do a certain thing? Why did they not do a different thing?

Position these discussions as requests for mentoring. Be open to learning as part of your assessment.

"WHY" is a powerful assessment tool. It is simple to observe behavior. It is also shallow. The magic is understanding the motivation for behavior. People can often say things they do not mean. They can sometimes "act" contrary to their beliefs. They can rarely describe the motivation for behavior in a meaningful way if the action was contrary to their belief structure.

When the pressure of day-to-day business activities occurs, leaders take action consistent with what they really believe. There is little opportunity for faking it for the sake of a message. True colors shine through in a person's unfiltered actions. These true colors take you beyond tone.

When you piece together enough WHY data points and behavior observations, patterns emerge. From that pattern you can make reasonable judgments about the leader's perspective on change. When you understand how they view change, you are a long way toward understanding if they, as leaders, are ready for the transformation you recommend.

Measure Openness

Following on from assessing the key leaders, you need to assess the organization's openness to change. Just as you assessed silo design elements in Chapter 3, here you are assessing the current state of your company's culture. This step is a broader observation of the company including the leaders' interaction within their teams and across the organization. Some of the data for this organizational assessment carries over from your leader assessment.

Your cultural assessment looks at how dynamic your organization is and how it has evolved. Your openness evaluation involves three primary elements:

- **Customer Lens**.
  Is the company truly customer- focused like we talk about in Chapter 19? Does the organization see its work through the lens of its customers? When a company has a true customer lens, it behaves based on the needs of others and not itself. The company takes on a servant's heart. The culture is "we" not "me."

  If your company truly has a heart for its customers, that is a strong indication it has the openness necessary to embrace the silos-to-pillars transformation – especially because the transformation is for the customers it serves.

- **Incremental/Transformational**.
  Is the company truly innovative to move itself in transformative ways or does it reluctantly take incremental improvement steps when forced to do so? This is a question of appetite for change. When a company only takes on incremental change, it likely holds on to the status quo with a death grip. Companies that embrace transformational change have a greater openness to change of all kinds.

  One warning here. Many confuse the speed of change with the nature of change. Some companies have great capacity to change things quickly. These quick change organization are often, however, making small and incremental changes out of necessity in response to crisis. Transformation, by its very nature, takes time. And while it may be perceived as slower, it is much more profound. If you must choose between fast and small versus slow and transformational, take the latter.

- **Idea Exchange**.
  Does staff initiate ideas? Does leadership listen? Idea exchange is a strong barometer of openness to change. If a company believes that only those in leadership have good ideas, there is likely little openness to change.

  If idea generation is limited to leadership, or even only executive leadership, then acceptable changes will be tied to the scope of executive leadership's vision and appetite for change. If ideas are welcomed from all, then there is an inherent openness to change because ideas come from every facet of the company.

  Companies that want the collective intelligence of their entire team are open to the direction that intelligence leads them. If only a small number of senior executives are deemed worthy to generate ideas, the company's future vision is constrained to a few "idea people." This constraint means the company is unlikely open to change of any meaningful magnitude.

Exploring these types of questions gives you a profile of your company's appetite to undertake the transformation you want to lead. Companies that view work from their own perspective, only

> When you get enough WHY data points and behavior observations, patterns emerge.

change incrementally and have little in the way of innovative dialogue with its employees are not good transformation candidates.

Identify Accountabilities

If you determine the leaders in your company seem supportive of transformation and your company seems open to transformation, you should be ready to go. Right? Wrong.

Your most important assessment is whether your organization has sufficient accountability infrastructure to support transforming silos into pillars. Assessing accountability infrastructure is as simple as asking the question "will the company enforce its decision to pursue the transformation I am seeking to lead?"

There are two important components to the question of accountability infrastructure and you must answer both components in the affirmative:

- **Is the company an accountability company?**
  The first element of the question is whether the company as a whole is accountable. Are people held to account for the things they are tasked with doing? Leadership should be driving objectives for members of the team consistent with the company's strategic goals. Equally, members of the team should take on the work assigned and be affirmatively accountable for its completion. If your company does not have such accountability, transformation will be difficult because there is a great deal of work to be done and if some are not up to the task, the effort will fail.

- **Will people be accountable to you?**
  This is a defining question in your assessment. Most of the accountability infrastructure occurs within your company's chain of command. The transformation you are recommending does not occur within the chain of command. As a Hub Leader, you will traverse across the organization as you lead the transformation. As

discussed above, you have little, if any, direct authority over those with whom you are working. Despite this, will the company position you, as leader of the transformation, in such a way that there is no room for dissent? Will you be given enough authority to exercise reasonable direction to those over whom you do not have chain of command authority? If not, you will not be successful.

If you determine that, despite the positive value of the silos-to-pillars transformation, your company is not ready, then you need to help create a different environment. We address that in the next chapter.

If you do not believe creating a different environment is possible, you can use the tools and tactics in this book to simply make your work more effective and look for a later time to begin transformation.

Chapter 17

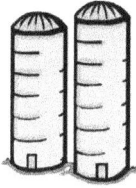

Create the Environment

"The best way to predict the future is to create it."

- Abraham Lincoln

Many organizations are not ready for the new thinking and work necessary to transform silos into pillars. Yet, you may believe the positive effect of the transformation outweighs your assessment there is a lack of readiness.

While your commitment is commendable, it is a fool's errand if you proceed in the face of the lack of readiness. If you believe transformation is the right course for your company right now, you need to do some work to reposition the organization and create an environment for success.

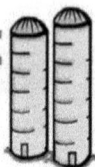

Resource Snapshot

change anything
Kerry Patterson, Joseph Grenny,
David Maxfield, Ron McMillan, and
Al Switzler

change anything looks at the science of changing yourself and those around you. The authors go well beyond the concept of will power to give clear direction on the specific action items necessary to grow yourself and move things forward in your personal and professional life.

Key Quote

"As you watch effective Changers in action, you note that in some form they learn to recognize their crucial moments, create vital behaviors, conduct a personal skill scan, discover where they have to learn new skills, and then work on them."

Website

www.vitalsmarts.com

Why this Resource?

If the Hub Leader cannot consistently change things at the beginning, in the middle and throughout the transformation of silos to pillars, success is fleeting.

www.silostopillars.com/resource-snapshot

Frame the Benefit

You have believed for quite some time in the positive impact of the silos-to-pillars transformation. For those with whom you speak, the transformation is brand new and somewhat a mystery. They may not get it. Many will not want to get it. You will certainly be viewed as the Heretic described in Chapter 20. To address this negativity and shape a more receptive environment, you must flip the script.

To flip the script, remember the word transformation can be both a verb and a noun. The verb, transform, focuses on the work to turn one thing into something else. The noun, transformation, focuses on the result of the work. In short, the noun is the outcome of the verb.

Discussing the work (verb) required to transform your company's silos into pillars is not an engaging topic. Everyone is busy. More work, no matter the benefit, is not attractive. Framing the benefit means discussing positive impact the transformation (noun) produces in customer satisfaction, operational excellence and elimination of risk. You discuss these outcomes as though they are already present. Which of these two statements do you think gets the more positive response?

"I'd like to talk about a transformation project that will help us have better operational performance and allow us to comply more effectively."

Or

"*I'd like to talk about ways we can reduce risk in our operation and better serve our customers.*"

While there is a possibility that neither gets an entirely positive response, the second statement has the better chance of a "Sure, let's chat" response. They offer to chat because they want the outcome.

Leaders want results. They want the needle to move. They want the outcome. They do not want the blood, sweat and tears. In the movie *Baby Boom*, J.C. Wiatt (played by Diane Keaton) is a former Wall Street executive who leaves the rat race and moves to an old house in Vermont with her newly adopted baby. In the dead of winter her water system breaks and she calls a plumber who tries to explain to her the problems with her water system and the work necessary to fix it. In an utterly complete emotional breakdown, Wiatt tells the plumber, "I just want to turn on the faucet to have water. I don't want to know where it's coming from!"

Your leaders want the same. If you need greater adoption of your transformation plan, do not sell the work, sell the result. Frame every discussion in terms of what positive outcomes the company can achieve. Whether its risk mitigation, greater insight into the operation or happier customers, let that be your focus. These are the things leaders want. Give them water when they turn on the faucet. They do not want or need to know how it works.

What if?

During the 1980s, computing giant Hewlett-Packard ran a national advertising campaign based on the simple question "What if?" The campaign's message was based on HP's commitment to partner with customers to solve their most important problems. "What if?" was the window to a world of possibilities that would bring positive results to HP's customers.

"What if?" is equally powerful for you. "What if?" gives you the chance to place your benefit front and center and make it a possibility. Good leaders are always looking for improvement possibilities. What catches their attention is the result. "What if?" speaks their language.

You can use "What if?" to do two important things. First, you can use it to gain buy-in from leaders about the transformation itself with engaging questions such as: "What if you had better risk data to keep the board informed?" "What if we could have greater insight into our performance while ensuring our compliance with customer requirements?" These are compelling questions. Good leaders are intrigued and want to know more.

"What if?" also opens the door to pursuing the transformation on a manageable scale. Remember, you are proposing something that is likely outside the norm for your organization. The transformation is

> *If you need greater adoption of your transformation plan, do not sell the work, sell the results.*

also outside the Leader's comfort zone. They do not want to be stained with a transformational failure. "What if?" gives you a way to initiate the transformation at low risk for the leader and high reward for your proposal.

In your assessment from Chapter 16, you should have identified potential champions for your transformation proposal. With these champions in mind, you have your run way.

Now your question shifts from "What if?" related to transformation benefit to "What if?" we could successfully prove the transformation with a certain department or work flow. This "What if?" provides you the opportunity to demonstrate the benefit and gives your leaders the protection of a small scale prototype. The prototype reduces the risk and encourages agreement.

Show the Benefit

You have sold the benefit and gained agreement to build a "What if?" prototype. It is time to execute. The rest of Part 5 talks about the tactical keys to execute. But before we go down that path, there is one more element to moving the environment - showing results.

Never forget that you are doing something outside the norm. You are changing the status quo. There will be those who do not like what you are doing or how you are doing it. As you sold this transformation on its benefits, you must commit to quantifying and showing the benefits on a regular basis. This commitment to reporting helps manage expectations.

Operations and Executive Leadership want a cadence of reporting to have ongoing understanding of the project's progress. The reporting gives a clear picture of the scope and pace of the work being performed. If Operations or Executive Leadership want to adjust the scope or pace, that opportunity is available through the reporting.

Showing the benefits is about metrics, key performance indicators and regular periodic reporting. Be generous with your reporting. Be transparent in what is working and what is not. Rather than trying to show everything works all the time, it is actually more powerful to show that something initially did not work and through continued effort the transformation turned things around.

You are vulnerable at this stage. It is your proposal. It is your transformation effort. Being open about its progress demonstrates the candor of your work and your confidence in its outcome. Show the benefits. Be clear about the obstacles. Be prepared to address contingencies to overcome the obstacles. In short, you want the leaders to understand you are fully committed to your proposal, you know how to execute it to success and you will do whatever is necessary to deliver the benefits you promised.

Through focusing on the transformation benefits, discussing "What if?" and showing the benefit, you should be able to create an environment in which leaders support your work to transform silos into pillars. This is likely not achieved in a single attempt. It likely will take a number of iterations to gain acceptance of the transformation effort you are leading. To achieve acceptance, the Hub Leader is consistent and vigilant. With consistent, well thought out efforts, you should find success.

One note of caution. Despite your best efforts, you may not ultimately be successful in persuading leaders to see the world differently. You may not be able to create an environment more prepared for transforming silos into pillars.

You simply cannot move forward into an unwelcoming environment. You will not be successful and you will your standing in the company. If you cannot create the environment needed, use your skills to make the current culture the best you can. Be part of the best of your company rather than a contrarian who thinks about how it should be. At a minimum, build the road maps we discussed in Chapter 3.

Chapter 18

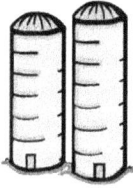

Start with Risk

"You cannot swim for new horizons until you have courage to lose sight of the shore."

- *William Faulkner*

  Risk kicks off all work weaving the Core Threads. Risk is the first step because it is the catalyst for everything in business. The first challenge is risk identification. Consider the 2000-year old parable of the Farmer and the Horse:

> *A Chinese farmer works his farm with his son and a horse. One day, the horse runs away. A neighbor hears of the horse running away and says to the farmer, "that's bad news."*
>
> *The farmer calmly replies, "Good news, bad news, who can say?"*
>
> *The horse comes back followed by a herd of horses that run into the farmer's corral. A neighbor sees the horse has returned, sees*

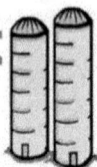

Resource Snapshot

Start With Why
Simon Sinek

Start With Why is focused on what inspires work. When one clearly answers the WHY question, then a flow of actions begins to occur. Teams buy-in. Customers buy. Sinek ties the importance of WHY directly to how human brains are wired. So, while some may try to persuade why WHY is important, Sinek ties it to biology.

Key Quote

"Manipulations can motivate the outcome of an election, but they don't help choose who should lead. To lead requires those who willingly follow. . . . To inspire starts with the clarity of WHY."

Website

www.startwithwhy.com

Why this Resource?

The Hub Leader must be able to articulate a clear WHY that resonates with Operations and Executive Leadership. Sinek's book helps with that clarity.

www.silostopillars.com/resource-snapshot

the farmer now has a number of additional horses and says to the farmer, "that is good news."

The farmer calmly replies, "Good news, bad news, who can say?" The farmer gives one of the horses to his son to ride. The horse throws the son who badly breaks his leg. A concerned neighbor tells the farmer how sorry he is for the bad news.

The farmer calmly replies, "Good news, bad news, who can say?"

A week later, the emperor's men come and take every able-bodied young man to fight in a war. The farmer's son is spared.

Good news, bad news, who can say?

This parable reveals two insights to risk: i) every circumstance has elements of risk and ii) risk can be an opportunity (good news) or threat (bad news). Identifying the risk and understanding the effect of the risk (opportunity or threat) sets great leaders apart.

The Hub Leader understands that risk is a constant. It exists in both Operations as well as the Core Threads. It presents itself in both the positive and negative of business. Beginning with risk gives the Hub Leader the perspective and insight to navigate the transformation successfully.

Risk is Business' Language

Risk is at the heart of all conversations in business. There is not a time when team members are not i) planning for a contingency; ii) identifying ways to fix problems or iii) strategizing about how to take advantage of an opportunity. Each of these discussions addresses risk.

If Hub Leaders do not make risk part of their language, they are ignoring a core element of their work. Ignoring the place risk holds in the business causes performance to suffer. Risk in a business is like gravity in the world. You do not have to believe in gravity. But, if you step off a high place, gravity makes its presence known.

The same is true of risk. There is no requirement to acknowledge risk in the operation of a business. There is no need to identify risks inherent in the processes a company uses to deliver goods and services to its customers. But, if there is no system by which to identify, mitigate, eliminate and treat the risks in your business, they still exist and will have a negative effect, whether you acknowledge the risk or not.

Make risk part of your conversations. Make it part of your planning. Make it part of the weaving of Core Threads into Operations. Becoming fluent in the language of risk ignites the silos-to-pillars transformation.

Risk Clarifies and Prioritizes

In the 1987 movie *Wall Street*, Gordon Gekko (played by Michael Douglas) extols the virtues of greed in his speech to the stockholders of the fictional company, Teldar Paper:

> *The point is, ladies and gentleman, that greed -- for lack of a better word -- is good. Greed is right. Greed works. Greed clarifies, cuts through, and captures the essence of the evolutionary spirit.*

While Gekko's opinion on greed may be a bit over the top, the same sort of argument may be made about risk.

Risk defines our interaction with the environment. Children are taught about risk from nearly the day they are born. "Don't touch that." "Watch for traffic." "Don't talk to strangers." Each of these, and dozens more teaching moments are the foundation for protecting children from the risks inherent in growing up.

As we grow older, we learn that risk is not always a yes/no proposition. Risk becomes something to which we adapt our behaviors. Risk also becomes something we accept in certain circumstances because, without risk, there is little reward in life. As T.S. Eliot said, "only those who will risk going too far can possibly find out how far one can go."

Taking risk fuels success. Refusal to take and adapt to risk obscures opportunity and results in failure. Risk also drives how the Core Threads are executed within a business. Where higher risk exists, greater monitoring and control is necessary. Lower risk requires less oversight.

> The Hub Leader understands that risk is a constant.

Customers look for systematic attention to risk from your company. They want assurance that you recognize the risks inherent in your company's operation and deploy systems and processes to address those risks. Even if your company has never failed to deliver on any customer need, customers still expect you to have systems to address risk.

You Exist Because of Risk

Think about your newest customer. Why do you think they began working with your company? The answer is simple: risk. The customer had a need to have something done or delivered as part of its work. The customer either could not deliver what was needed or believed you could deliver it better. Risk of failure on their end caused the connection to your company to mitigate or eliminate their risk. In fact, all businesses exist because of risk. Businesses either i) help other businesses deliver or ii) provide goods and services to people who need them. In either case, problems (risks) are solved.

Everything cannot be risk, can it? Isn't this just a bit dramatic? Not really. Even mundane things you buy because of risk. Groceries? Risk of starvation. Gasoline? Risk of being stranded. Risk of not getting where you need to be. Haircut? Risk of not being attractive to others. Oil change? Risk of car malfunctioning. The list goes on and on. Focusing on risk as the catalyst for business keeps your approach consistent.

As you explore how to weave, remember why you weave. The Hub Leader weaves the Core Threads to protect Operations from risk to ensure fulfilling customer needs. We weave to strengthen Operations. That strength helps address customer's risk. We weave so the company is sustainable, avoids the risk of failure and is ready to capitalize on the risks of opportunity.

Your customers selected your company to solve one or more of their risks. Your company's delivery on that risk solution is vital to your customer's ability to deliver. You can bet your customers will assess your company. On what will they assess you? Risk. Their risk. Customer's risk review inevitably arises because your customer views your company as a risk.

Start with risk. It's why you exist.

Chapter 19

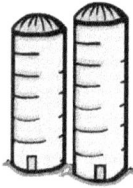

Create a Customer Lens

"We see our customers as invited guests to a party, and we are the hosts."

- Jeff Bezos

Customers are the lifeblood of every business. Have too few and your business is short-lived. Have too many and . . . well, you have a good problem to solve.

There is an ever-growing focus on how to take care of customers more effectively. What is interesting is this focus on customer care is about thirty years old.

Prior to the last thirty years, businesses were largely focused on marketing and advertising to persuade customers to buy. Today's focus is on how to serve customers so they stay after the buy. The ever-expanding choices customers have makes customer retention as important as customer acquisition. This requires business to design not only systems to get customers to buy, but also

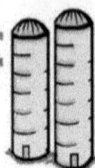

Resource Snapshot

Outside In
Steve Towers

Outside In is a roadmap for optimizing customer experience as part of a company delivering "successful customer outcomes." Towers condenses his decades of work into a simple to follow blueprint of i) moments of truth; ii) hand overs and iii) business rules to address customer expectations on a sustainable and repeatable basis.

Key Quote
"It [the secret] is about organizing ourselves around the person who pays our salary and keeps the shareholders happy – the customer."

Website
www.bpgroup.org

Why this Resource?
Transforming silos into pillars is an innovation designed to strengthen the company's connection to its customer. Towers' book adds a proven method to simplify that connection.

www.silostopillars.com/resource-snapshot

systems to meet customer expectations after the sale to ensure they continue to buy.

As a Hub Leader working with the Core Threads, your lens is the customer. The Core Threads are not programs deployed to give your business a warm and fuzzy feeling. The Core Threads are for customers to create an enduring trust in your business. That trust is at the heart of the customer experience that supports a sustainable relationship.

Customer Focus or Lens?

There is a tremendous difference between a company that proclaims "we do everything our customers want" and one that says "we deliver based on our customer's needs." The first statement is customer focus. The second is a customer lens. Two elements in the statements illustrate the focus versus lens difference.

The first is the use of the word <u>want</u> versus <u>need</u>. Many may see little difference between the two words. In fact, there is a great deal of difference. Wants are often the product of giving customers limitless choices without context related to what your company delivers.

Henry Ford understood wants when he said "if I had asked my customers what they wanted, they would have said faster horses." Companies may truly focus on their customers when they do what their customers want. But, in doing so, are they serving their customers' needs -- even those needs of which their customers are unaware? Perhaps not.

Customer needs are a very different thing altogether. Customer needs arise in the context of what your company delivers. Henry Ford knew the population of the United States would become more mobile in the early part of the 20th century. With this new mobility, effective mechanical transportation would be needed. Ford surmised horses would no longer be sufficient for a large portion of the population. He envisioned a need materializing.

Ford did not build automobiles because he thought people wanted automobiles. Ford built automobiles because he knew people needed reliable transportation beyond that of a horse. Ford did not have a customer focus. He was largely uninterested in wants. He showed this when he said, "a customer can have a car painted any color he wants as long as it's black." Ford had a lens into what his customers would need and reshaped personal transportation with a company that continues to this day.

The second difference is a bit more subtle. The first statement talks about what a business does ("what our customers want"). The second statement stresses alignment ("based on our customer's needs"). Aligning the company's processes with the customer's needs moves beyond focus to a lens.

There is nothing wrong with doing what a customer wants. In fact, virtually every business does this every day. But, if the company's focus is primarily on doing what the customer wants, then the company is leaving its evolution up to its customers who are largely indifferent about its success. Think of it this way. Who knows best what your company can and should do? The answer is not your customer.

The magic of the second statement is that the work the company delivers is <u>designed</u> and <u>delivered</u> to address the customer's needs. This involves your company having superior knowledge of and insight to your customer's business. From there, you can take the skills of your business and build unique, forward-thinking processes that address those customer needs with sustainable precision.

Steve Jobs, founder of Apple, captured this customer lens idea when he said, "begin with the customer experience and work back to the technology." Jobs understood the strongest customer relationships began with Apple intimately understanding customers' needs and how they interacted (or would interact) with Apple's products. From there, Apple designed through that customer experience lens. Simply put, no one knew they needed an iPhone until Apple produced the first one. Now, millions of customers cannot imagine not having one.

As a Hub Leader, you need to develop that customer lens. You need to be a student of your customers, their needs and how they interact with your company and its products/services. From that customer experience knowledge, you design your work to meet those needs, whether your customers know these needs exist or not. You have two customers for whom you do this analysis and design: i) Operations and ii) your company's customers. When you understand each customer's experience and deliver based on their needs, you have a customer lens.

Customers Expect Core Threads

Why does your company exist? Customers. Why does your company do the work it does? Customers. If there is no customer, there is no business. All work is performed for the customer.

This is an important point for the Hub Leader to remember. None of the Core Threads are woven into Operations for the sake of the company. They are woven for the sake of the customer because all work done in Operations is for the customer.

Hub Leaders remain relevant and engaged with Operations based on customer needs. Hub Leaders do not work for their own credit. They do not weave for the

> But, if the company's focus is primarily on doing what the customer wants, then the company is leaving its evolution up to its customers who are largely indifferent about its success.

sake of the company. The Hub Leader shepherds the transformation of silos into pillars for the sake of the customer.

Many times Operations staff resist the Core Threads by arguing the customer does not care about Core Threads. This is simply wrong. As discussed above, customers choose your company to mitigate or eliminate risk in their business. In doing so, your customer trades the risk they faced before choosing your company for the risk of working with your company.

Now that your company is the risk, your customer assesses your company's systems and processes dedicated to reducing or eliminating risk in your delivery. Your customer evaluates your company on issues of risk management, quality, information security and compliance to name a few. They assess your systems and, in many cases, make findings and recommendations to strengthen those systems.

Far from not caring about the Core Threads, your customers demand them.

Connect Core Threads to Customers

Customers' demand for the Core Threads supports the path for the Hub Leader's work. Again, the focus is exclusively on customers and their requirements. When you approach Operations with Core Thread work, it is based on connecting that work to customer needs.

Operations is singularly focused on delivery to the customer. Operations embraces the Core Threads when the Hub Leader effectively connects the Core Threads directly to that same delivery. You also have client and regulatory assessments as a further connection that reminds all that weaving the Core Threads deeply into Operations is key to delivering on customer needs.

Chapter 20

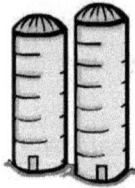

Secure All Sides

"Engage your brain before you engage your weapon."

- Gen. James Mattis, U.S. Sec. of Defense

While General Mattis' quote applies to soldiers, it applies equally to the Hub Leader weaving Core Threads within and throughout the silos of a business. General Mattis advocates preparation at all times to execute your mission. For the Hub Leader, that means being prepared for the contingencies that can affect the mission of transforming silos into pillars.

The Hub Leader starts with risk because that is the language of business and drives everything that should be done in that business. Next, the Hub Leader designs activities focused exclusively through a customer lens. This design is essential because the business exists for the

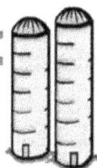

Resource Snapshot

Buy-In
John P. Kotter and Lorne A. Whitehead

Buy-In addresses that most fragile phase of an idea – after inception and before implementation. Kotter and Whitehead focus an entire book on the tactics and techniques to ensure that an idea survives the gauntlet of nay-sayers, enemies and people who simply resist change.

Key Quote
"You need to win hearts and minds to get buy-in. Simple, clear, and commonsense responses can do much to win the minds. Respect can do much to win hearts."

Website
www.kotterinternational.com/buyin

Why this Resource?
The Hub Leader's greatest challenge is buy-in. Kotter and Whitehead present a wonderful guide to overcome that challenge.

www.silostopillars.com/resource-snapshot

customer and all work of the business is for the customer.

Risk and customer focus are design elements the Hub Leader controls. The Hub Leader does not need buy in from anyone to address risk or commit to a customer lens. Others will not object to managing risk or delivering on customer needs.

General Mattis' advice becomes important after risk and customer lens. The Hub Leader's next step in the transformation plan is to execute within the organization. Buy-in is now front and center. This means the Hub Leader executes a thorough review and understanding of the Hub Leader's surroundings. From this assessment, the Hub Leader can prepare General Mattis' "plan" to remain safe from harm.

Map the Top (i.e., who's with me?)

The Hub Leader is not the CEO of an organization. A CEO has far too much responsibility to take the lead on weaving Core Threads. This means the Hub Leader has accountability to someone (or many) in driving the silo transformation. Understanding how those to whom the Hub Leader is accountable view i) the Core Threads, ii) their integration into Operations and iii) the proposed transformation gives the Hub Leader a barometer of how to proceed.

Mapping the top is different from the euphemistic "Tone at the Top." Tone at the Top often centers on top management being a cheerleader for particular activities. While the Hub Leader can always use an ally in executive management that is not the map the Hub Leader is drawing.

The Hub Leader first map points involve an understanding of who in Operations is likely a supporter and who is not. Armed with this data, the Hub Leader adds map points related to executive leaders' view of the transformation gathered through discussions of the proposed approach to the transformation. These discussions are frank and positive. The Hub Leader focuses on how to be most effective and least disruptive in weaving the Core Threads and achieving transformation.

From these discussions, the Hub Leader has a number of map points that create a clear vision of leadership's view of and commitment to transforming silos into pillars. This discussion may signal a need to continue working with leadership to increase understanding and support. If reasonable support is present, the Hub Leader proceeds.

Bolt the Back (i.e., who's against me?)

The Hub Leader also discusses the proverbial back door with leadership. All who have worked in business for any length of time are aware of how devastating it is to have someone go through the back door to sabotage a project. The Hub Leader takes great pains to bolt the back door closed from the inside.

To bolt the back means having clear "rules of engagement" related to the Hub Leader's work. The Hub Leader acknowledges that weaving the Core Threads may disrupt Operations. The Hub Leader designs and executes the transformation work to minimize or eliminate such disruption. Yet, Operations will still resist the change.

Bolting the back addresses when Operations tries to sabotage the transformation,

Earlier we talked about resistance to the Hub Leader's work. Bolting the back is one of the ways the Hub Leader neutralizes resistance through a backdoor attack. The Hub Leader needs a commitment from leaders that a backdoor attack will not derail the transformation. If Operations has a concern about disruption, that can be addressed. The Hub Leader commits to alter, delay or otherwise change any activities that create unacceptable disruption. Leaders agree any other attack is resistance and will not derail the Hub Leader's work.

This does not mean the Hub Leader advocates that the Executive Leader refuse to listen to Operations' concerns. Quite the contrary. Operations' concerns are of critical importance to the Hub Leader's success. The concerns show what is not work and, hopefully, why. The Hub Leader wants commitment from leaders to be engaged to address every complaint, every resistance and every push back on the work of weaving the Core Threads. It is only through having this information and being engaged in the discussion that the Hub Leader adapts to the concerns. It is the opportunity to adapt the Core Thread activities out of respect for the silo and its team.

But in the end, the Hub Leader wants the security of knowing the back door is bolted and under no circumstances is that door to be opened without the Hub Leader's engagement.

See the Front

The front represents where the organization is going. Businesses are highly dynamic. Things go from good to bad and back very quickly. The Hub Leader keeps a forward eye on the organization, its strategy and its current state of operation. It is the front that governs the Hub Leader's pace and direction.

When the organization is operating in harmony and alignment, the Hub Leader's work focuses on advancement. This is the time when weaving Core Threads into legacy operational processes occurs. Operations is more open to the collaboration because things are running smoothly and the Hub Leader's work is less of a distraction to Operations getting the work out the door.

The Hub Leader is sensitive when Operations is struggling. When Operations is struggling, the Hub Leader shifts from advancement to support. While in the time of harmony, the Hub Leader seeks to move forward with

> To bolt the back door means having clear "rules of engagement" related to the Hub Leader's work.

weaving in legacy processes, in less optimal times, the Hub Leader evaluates existing weaves to offer solutions to Operations. It is this shift in focus that keeps the Hub Leader in the foxhole with Operations and brings true value on the road back to harmony.

The third state of the business is transformation. Growth, innovation and new processes are at the heart of this time. The Hub Leader plays a key role in times of transformation through being part of the design team. The Hub Leader strengthens process at the time of initial design which makes deployment more successful. The Hub Leader stands side-by-side with Operations to design the Core Threads intuitively into the new, transformative processes.

Don't Run to Your Death

The Navy Seals are one of the most elite fighting units on the planet. They execute covert operations all over the world with precision and tenacity. They live by a code of honor that distinguishes them to friend and foe. "Don't run to your death" is a Seal mantra that is of profound importance to the Hub Leader. While it may be counterintuitive, the Seals believe that the closer one gets to a target, the slower and more deliberate one should move. This applies equally to Hub Leaders.

Navy Seals do not execute missions from long range. They are often face-to-face with their enemy. In a June 30, 2014 post on *Inc.com*, author Brent Gleeson, a retired Seal, describes this Seal mantra as follows:

> *When conducting raids that put you in close-quarters combat scenarios, restraint is often the best approach. Once you breach and gain entry to the target, being slow and methodical often wins the race. Hence the phrase, "Don't run to your death."*

The Hub Leader works in the same close quarters with Operations. As the Hub Leader works to become a trusted advisor and identifies the opportunities to help weave the Core Threads, there is a potential shot of adrenaline to jump in and make big strides. Resist those urges.

The Hub Leader's goal is long term, sustainable improvement through integrating Core Threads into operational processes. This is not a sprint; it is a marathon that requires dedication and resolve. While moving quickly may make a splash, it may also flame out, damage your relationship with Operations and slow your overall progress. Restraint and a methodical approach to achieve the mission keeps the Hub Leader in the game and avoids death to the trusted advisor relationship central to success.

Chapter 21

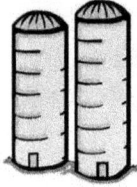

Design Past the Rough Patch

"People don't resist change. They resist being changed!"

- Peter Senge

The real challenge in change management is not the change but the management. There is certainly enough challenge to the buy-in for the transformation. Once initiated, there are human factors that substantially affect the successful transformation.

The Hub Leader is a talented change agent. Managing that change is a vital Hub Leader skill. As the Hub Leader integrates the Core Threads deeper and deeper into silos, greater management is required because more people are involved. The Hub Leader that masters the management of change becomes the master Core Threads weaver who drives transformation.

Resource Snapshot

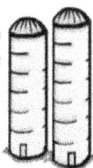

Switch
Chip Heath and Dan Heath

Switch focuses on overcoming the challenges leaders face in executing change. The Heaths' focus, however, is on how change affects the mind and how the brain resists change. This gives insight into how a leader designs change efforts to more effectively reach the next place.

Key Quote
"For things to change, somebody somewhere has to start acting differently. Maybe it's you, maybe it's your team."

Website
www.heathbrothers.com/books/switch

Why this Resource?
A Hub Leader needs to understand the obstacles to change and how to overcome them. *Switch* gives insight into the invisible challenges the mind presents to change and provides a method to address these challenges.

www.silostopillars.com/resource-snapshot

Managing Change is Crucial

The Hub Leader provokes change. This provocation itself presents a challenge. The challenge is heightened because the change is not directed at broken operational processes. Rather, the change is focused on integrating the Core Threads design elements into what are likely well-performing operational processes.

Sometimes the Hub Leader's work faces the "if it ain't broke, don't fix it" argument. In fact, in many cases the Hub Leader is not fixing at all. The Hub Leader is working to strengthen and improve process. All of this requires change of thought, change of perspective and, in some cases, change in behavior. Underpinning all of it, the changes require management.

The Hub Leader focuses on how best to help Operations move from where it is to where it needs to be. This effort requires thorough planning, engaging with Operations leaders and working deliberately to keep things moving forward (even if not at the pace the Hub Leader had envisioned).

Going back to Senge's quote, the Hub Leader manages the human element of change as much as the process change itself. The Hub Leader helps those impacted to be part of the solution. The Hub Leader has specific outcomes that the changes are meant to achieve. Sharing those outcomes and seeking input helps avoid the feeling of "being changed." It also may unearth a better approach. If the Hub Leader leaves Operations out, it will not feel like part of the solution. It will feel more like a victim of the solution rather than a part of the solution.

The business of change is driven by the challenge of figuring out how to perform the process with the new design elements. The gap to that new state exists because the current processes are not designed to do the new thing.

The Hub Leader works with affected staff on the process design to convert the future how into the now. The now is the process, newly designed, integrated with the Core Threads to achieve optimized outcomes. Thus, while change is inevitable, driving change is intentional.

Change is the Rough Patch

No matter how much planning and no matter how deliberate the Hub Leader acts, change causes the road to be rough. This is unavoidable. Road construction offers a great example. Crews work on sections of roads as projects progress. The road leading to the construction zone is smooth; the construction zone is rough. After the construction zone, the road smooths out again.

This is how organizational change works. The rough patch should not be a discouragement. As noted above, when change begins, the people and processes affected

> *All of this requires change of thought, change of perspective and, in some cases, change in behavior.*

are not designed to do the new thing. The Hub Leader's job is to collaborate with affected groups on an improved design and implement that design in the construction zone until the road smooths.

Navigating Operations through the rough patch is part of the value the Hub Leader delivers. It's simple to see the value in change. It is simple to plan change and initiate change. The challenge is to see the change through in an effective and positive way. It is the true Hub Leader that stays the course and works through the change to get Operations to the new smooth road.

The Three Stages of Truth

There are countless resources regarding change management. Some are philosophical about managing the human reaction to change. Others are more tactical and give a how-to for change management. One of my favorites, Switch, featured in this chapter's Resource Snapshot, touches both sides of this equation. This section touches on a way a Hub Leader tracks progress through the change management process.

Change management is like changing an idea or a truth. Understanding how people adopt new ideas or truths lays a path for the Hub Leader to monitor for progress. The three stages of truth identify the evolution of people's reaction to a new truth from inception to acceptance. Change management is little more than the process of moving people from one way of thinking (or doing) to another. In other words, presenting, persuading and institutionalizing a new idea or truth.

The three stages of truth date back to at least 1818 and German philosopher Arthur Schopenhauer. In a more modern version of the stages, University of California Santa Cruz anthropologist Adrienne Zihlman describes the stages as follows:

It has been said that the reception of any successful new scientific hypothesis goes through three predictable phases before being accepted. First, it is criticized for being untrue. Secondly, after supporting evidence accumulates, it is stated that it may be true, but it is not particularly relevant. Thirdly, after it has clearly influenced the field, it is admitted to be true and relevant, but the same critics assert that the idea was not original.

The Hub Leader uses these very simply stages of truth to track the team's progress along the path to change.

- **Stage 1 - The Heretic**

    George Bernard Shaw said that "all great truths begin as blasphemies." There was a time when it was generally accepted i) the Earth was the center of the universe; ii) the Earth was flat and iii) humans could not engage in sustained flight. Copernicus, Newton and Wright proved each of these beliefs wrong. Initial responses to these works was highly negative and sometimes brought severe consequences to those visionaries espousing those beliefs.

    A heretic is someone who holds an opinion about something that is at odds with what is the generally accepted view. This is precisely what the Hub Leader does. The idea that the Core Threads can be integrated into operational process to turn silos into pillars is contrary to generally accepted views. The Hub Leader should anticipate the label.

    The Hub Leader knows the chosen path is correct. The initial negative response against the Hub Leader's ideas confirms it is the right path. If you know your course to be correct, you must push past this initial heretic stage.

- **Stage 2 - The Gnat**

    The second stage of truth begins when others respond "it may be true, but it is no big deal." Stage two begins to show a glimmer of acceptance of the Hub Leader's work. The challenge for the Hub Leader is recognizing the progress and not becoming discouraged.

When the people around you are characterizing your work as "no big deal", it is easy to become disheartened and slow execution. To the contrary, the Hub Leader needs to respond with even more vigor to execute the work. Those with whom the Hub Leader is working have acknowledged the correctness of the path. The fact they may minimize its value or impact is unimportant. Continue to push. The big impact exists whether others want to acknowledge it or not.

The second stage of truth offers the Hub Leader an added bonus. Because those working with the Hub Leader see the ideas as "no big deal", it protects the Hub Leader from total resistance. In other words, if the work is no big deal and does not distract Operations from producing, it is doubly hard for Operations to keep the Hub Leader from making progress.

When you hit stage two, accelerate; do not slow down.

- **Stage 3 – The Follower**
  Stage 3 is when all around the Hub Leader say, believe they knew it all along and this is how we have always done it. When this becomes the group's belief, you have successfully changed the thinking and the behavior. The challenge for the Hub Leader is to resist reminding the group that they did not, in fact, know this all along.

  It is tempting to recount the work you had to do to plant the seeds of those new ideas in their minds to evolve their thinking and behavior. You will hear some of those with the greatest resistance to your ideas quoting them as long-standing truths. Tools and techniques you recommended for weeks, months and maybe years are now being discussed as though they were always part of Operations.

Resist the temptation to set everyone straight. It won't work. It undermines your success. When the ideas and things you have promoted as the Hub Leader become the accepted norm, you have succeeded. You have delivered as you promised. The only thing left for you to do is have a knowing smile when others discuss your ideas as though they are their own.

You Will Find Smooth Road, Again

It is easy to become discouraged in the midst of change. There is resistance, conflict, doubt and moments of failure. Your job as the Hub Leader is to see past the rough patch of change to the smooth road of the newly embedded truth. As the business axiom goes, the Hub Leader engages in "gentle pressure, relentlessly applied." That pressure remains until success is achieved.

Beyond the pressure, however, the Hub Leader must keep the vision of the new day with the smooth road in front of those engaging in the change. Just as the continuing change can be discouraging to the Hub Leader, it can be more discouraging (and likely frustrating) to those experiencing the change. You must be the beacon of light and hope to a greater tomorrow. This is how you will find a smooth road, again.

Take Action

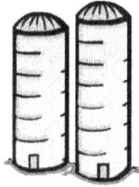

Chapter 22

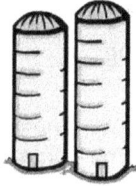

Start Where You Are

"Just where you are -- that's the place to start."

- Pema Chodron

You have done the legwork to understand how silos are really pillars in disguise. You have shifted from pour to dip mentality. Hub Leadership is your mantra and you understand how to weave. Now it is time to act.

Many look for the right time to act. Some look for the right circumstances. Others may look for the right season in the business to move forward. Tennis star Arthur Ashe said it best. "Start where you are. Use what you have. Do what you can." That is great advice. Hub Leaders start where they are because they have nowhere else to start.

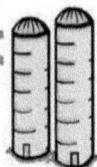

Resource Snapshot

The Reinventors
Jason Jennings

The Reinventors is about transformation. Jennings lays out how companies can "pursue radical continuous change." From letting go of the past through identification and systemization of the future, *The Reinventors* is a repeatable cycle to support ongoing, transformational change.

Key Quote
"The main job of a leader is to be a destination expert, to let everyone know where the company is going and make certain that everyone understands and is willing to embrace constant change in order to get there."

Website
www.jennings-solutions.com

Why this Resource?
Hub Leaders transform constantly. *The Reinventors* provides a guide to do so effectively.

www.silostopillars.com/resource-snapshot

Think Like a Contractor

We've spent a good portion of this book talking about the importance of relationships. This section may sound counter that message. It is not. This section embraces the relationship message and provides counsel on how to structure relationships more effectively as a Hub Leader. The relationship focus for the Hub Leader involves connection with Operations. Thinking like a contractor is how the Hub Leader approaches those relationships.

Contractors service clients. Hub Leaders serve Operations. Contractors have no illusion they will take over their client's work. Hub Leaders do not envision taking over Operations. Contractors build tools, provide guidance and assist clients in achieving the client's goals. Hub Leaders do the same for Operations.

There are three reasons why Hub Leaders think like a contractor: i) it forces the Hub Leader to deliver with Operations and not to Operations (remember Pour versus Dip?); ii) it keeps the Hub Leader working exclusively from facts and avoids analyzing intentions and iii) it points the Hub Leader to helping, not intervening.

We have talked about Pour versus Dip. Thinking like a contractor helps the Hub Leader stay focused on integration through Dip Mentality. Contractors do work within the contractor's expertise that customers need for the customer's benefit. Under no circumstances do contractors work for their own benefit. Hub Leaders should not do work for their own benefit, either.

When Hub Leaders work with a company, they get to know Operations leaders. Through that relationship, the Hub Leader can take a wrong turn and begin assessing the intentions behind leaders' actions and inactions. The Hub Leader can take those actions and inactions personally as though designed to foil the Hub Leader's project (see the discussion in Chapter 9 of fundamental attribution error). Contractors do not care about intentions. Contractors care about doing the things necessary to achieve their mission. Hub Leaders should do the same.

Contractors want to achieve positive results to create satisfied customers. That is their formula for success. That formula is designed to create satisfied customers and attract additional opportunities. Hub Leaders, who think like contractors, have the same formula.

> *Hub Leaders start where they are because they have nowhere else to start.*

Identify what Operations needs (or what you have been charged to do). Get buy-in on the mission. Deliver the tools and support necessary to achieve the mission. Don't try to change Operations. Give the support needed to position Operations to achieve the change they seek. Done properly, this formula leads to the Hub Leader having more opportunities to serve.

Get a Clear Understanding of Current State

You have to know two things to map a journey of any kind: i) where you are going and ii) where you are. Without both, a successful journey is impossible.

Hub Leaders guide an organization on a journey to weave Core Threads into Operations and transform silos into pillars. Before beginning the journey, the Hub Leader takes stock of the company's current state.

Earlier we discussed assessing the silos to understand their design and delivery within the organization. This is part of the current state the Hub Leader evaluates. The current state also involves the strategic goals and objectives of the organization as a whole as well as within each operational unit.

An interesting byproduct of review of corporate and business unit goals demonstrates whether alignment exists within the organization. Having done the review, the Hub Leader may be in a position to help identify and solve any misalignment.

The Hub Leader needs a clear and complete picture of the organization's current state. What works? What does not work? Who are the leaders? Who has authority? Only with this clear snapshot of today can the Hub Leader act toward tomorrow.

Envision Future State

In Lewis Carroll's *Alice in Wonderland*, there is an exchange between the Cheshire Cat and Alice that illustrates the need for a well-defined destination:

Alice: Would you tell me, please, which way I ought to go from here?

The Cheshire Cat: That depends a good deal on where you want to get to.

Alice: I don't much care where.

The Cheshire Cat: Then it doesn't much matter which way you go.

The Cheshire Cat is right. Until Alice has a clear destination, the path is of no consequence. Equally, the Hub Leader must have a well-defined destination for the Core Threads and silo transformation. Without this clear destination, there is no map to ensure the Hub Leader and organization remain on track to completion. Just like Alice, if the Hub Leader has no destination, the path is meaningless and the likelihood of failure increases.

The Hub Leader remains adaptive in traveling the path to transformation. The future state is not something set in stone. It is a target to be used in the planning and execution of the Hub Leader's work. It is also a target to be routinely evaluated as the Hub Leader's work progresses. There may come a time that the future state target needs to be reevaluated.

Re-evaluation is an important thing for the Hub Leader. It recognizes that your business and the environment in which it works is dynamic. Changes are likely. These changes may signal a change is needed for the Hub Leader.

While in re-evaluation, the Hub Leader should slow work awaiting the assessment outcome. Working without a target creates drift of purpose. Once the target is established, the Hub Leader can resume pursuit of the transformation.

Draw Lines of Progress

Humans are incredibly adaptable creatures. As discussed earlier in the three stages of truth, a new idea eventually becomes the long held belief of those who so violently opposed it in the beginning. The Hub Leader draws lines of progress as bread crumbs to mark the evolution of thought and behavior.

Drawing lines of progress focuses on remembering how things were in the past so improvement can be identified and measured. As weaving the Core Threads proceeds, staff comes to believe the Core Threads design has always been part of their work. That is a great thing and should be a primary goal for the Hub Leader. That adoption, however, creates a loss of memory in the team of how things were and how far they have come. The Hub Leader keeps track of that progress.

Lines of progress also protect the Hub Leader and those with whom the Hub Leader works. Hub Leaders and their teams often have a forward-only vision of their work. They push through each obstacle to weaving the Core Threads with a singular view of the next goal to achieve. Each new goal brings new challenges and exposes gaps that need to be addressed. Again, this lean forward approach is good for the Hub Leader, those with whom the Hub Leader works and the organization as a whole.

The forward-only view also presents a serious risk. Transforming silos into pillars is not a destination, it is a process. It is a continuing and evolving process of i) moving a silo; ii) the silo adapting to the move and iii) moving the silo again by continuing to weave Core Threads. There are always improvements to pursue. The Hub Leader always pushes the envelope to continue the transformation. The work evolves; it never ends.

Lines of progress help give context to the work. At times, the Hub Leader, the team and the organization must look back and celebrate the progress. When work is focused on the continuing improvement of the organization, there needs to be an acknowledgement of the progress made to date. This reduces the risk of burnout and provides a renewed energy to the tasks at hand. With that renewed energy, all can continue the upward evolution of the silos-to-pillars transformation.

Chapter 23

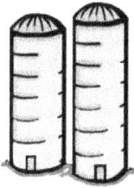

Deliver Your Value Proposition

"Strive not to be a success, but rather to be of value."

- *Albert Einstein*

Hub Leaders are not cogs in a wheel. They are not a box on an organizational chart. Hub Leader is a unique role undertaken by committed leaders that has its own unique challenges and rewards. The Hub Leader stands apart within the organization and occupies a unique position related to Operations.

This role demands that the Hub Leader stand for and deliver a value proposition. There is no standard value proposition which a Hub Leader must adopt. Each Hub Leader defines a value proposition based on the passion, focus and strengths brought to the position and the customers'/organization's needs.

Resource Snapshot

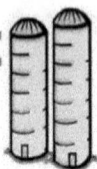

Made to Stick
Chip Heath and Dan Heath

Made to Stick is a walk through what makes ideas endure. It focuses on how to take a new and novel message or approach and develop it in such a way that it is remembered. Unlike many books on marketing, this one sets out a proven formula. It gives the reader the lenses through which to design, evaluate and implement great new ideas.

Key Quote
"If you want to spread your ideas to other people, you should work within the confines of the rules that have allowed other ideas to succeed over time. You want to invent new ideas, not new rules."

Website
www.madetostick.com

Why this Resource?
When the Hub Leader offers the idea of transforming silos to pillars, understanding how to make that idea stick is crucial.

www.silostopillars.com/resource-snapshot

You are a Product

Throughout this book we have explored the one-of-a-kind deliverables of a Hub Leader. What should have come through these points is that you, the Hub Leader, are a product within your organization. Thinking of yourself as a product helps increase your effectiveness.

To better understand the concept of Hub Leader as a product, we return to Tom Peters' book, *Re-imagine!*. Peters discusses business in the 21st century will be driven by what he calls PSFs (Professional Service Firms) embedded throughout an organization. Peters sees it this way:

> *We must destroy "departments" -- and create aggressive, imaginative, entrepreneurial Professional Service Firms (PSFs) in their stead. We must embrace PSFs as the Primary Engines for Creative Work . . . and thus of virtually all Enterprise Value Added.*

This is precisely what the Hub Leader is challenged to do. Leverage the discipline and structure of operational silos to weave Core Threads through and among those silos. This effort is delivered from a PSF-designed role that provides value to Operations which, in turn, delivers value to customers.

Peters call these "WOW Projects" and defines their characteristics as:

- *Projects that Matter*
- *Projects that Make a Difference*
- *Projects that you can Brag About . . . forever*
- *Projects that Transform the Enterprise*
- *Projects that Take Your Breath Away*
- *Projects that make you/me/us/"them" Smile*

- *Projects that Highlight the Value that you Add . . . and Why .
  . . You Are Here on Earth. (Yes, That Big.)*
- *WOW Projects are . . . not hype*
- *WOW Projects are . . . a necessity. (New Necessity.)*

If you can commit to deliver WOW, you can be a Hub Leader who transforms silos into pillars.

WIIFM

The Hub Leader is routinely selling i) the Core Threads, ii) the weaving of the Core Threads and iii) the transformation of silos into pillars. When navigating through the organization and across silos to carry the Core Threads' message, the acronym top of mind for the Hub Leader is WIIFM -- *What's In It For Me.*

Hub Leaders know Operations is not waiting for them to show up. In fact, Operations usually hopes you do not show up. It sees you as a distraction. It perceives you as the proverbial "thorn in their side." You will not find a welcome mat at Operations' door. You may find a "Keep Out" sign.

To gain entry (and not get thrown out), the Hub Leader focuses the work on the value brought to Operations. Although the Core Threads work is right for the business, the work must always be packaged correctly for Operations.

If at any point Operations leaders perceive there is nothing in it for them, your work is done. Your work may begin again if you can reposition it to demonstrate value to Operations (i.e., when there is something in it for Operations). Until then, you are dead in the water.

Never forget WIIFM.

Execute on Immediate Value Opportunities

The Hub Leader works toward a mission – the future state of silos transformed into pillars. This is an all-encompassing mission bringing great value to Operations and its customers.

Throughout the project, however, the Hub Leader needs to be aware of "value opportunities." Value opportunities are circumstances where progress and solutions can be delivered in specific, discreet areas.

A particular process may be exposed as needing an upgrade. A gap may be present that needs to be closed. No matter what it is, the circumstance gives the Hub Leader a way to produce specific value for Operations along the path to the ultimate mission.

> *Every Hub Leader must define a value proposition based on the passion, focus and strengths brought to the position and the customers'/organization's needs.*

Be on the lookout for these opportunities. Embrace a quick turn to these specific issues when present. Use these opportunities to show on a small scale what can be delivered on a large scale.

From these opportunities, Operations and Executive Leadership gains confidence in you and your work. Value opportunities, successfully executed, provide the evidence to which the Hub Leader can point to demonstrate what mission success will bring.

Master the Shifting Sands

After you know the current state and have identified the targeted future state, you face the challenge of the shifting sands. The shifting sands occur because what the Hub Leader "knows" changes. In the movie *Men in Black*, K (played by Tommy Lee Jones) tell his recruit J (played by Will Smith), "Five hundred years ago, everybody knew that the Earth was flat. And fifteen minutes ago, you knew that humans were alone on this planet. Imagine what you'll know tomorrow."

No matter how much planning a Hub Leader does, there are things that remain unknown and the sands of the project will shift. They may shift minute by minute or week by week; but, they will shift. As the Hub Leader progresses, new facts find their way to the surface. These new facts can change the Hub Leader's understanding of the current state. New facts may also clarify that the chosen path is not quite right.

The learning a Hub Leader goes through while working in and among the silos is profound. Beyond the objective facts, the successful Hub Leader becomes more intimately aware of Operations' work as well as the leaders and staff within Operations.

Done well, the Hub Leader's work creates a new openness from Operations that brings greater clarity to the Hub Leader. Do not be frustrated with the new facts. Embrace them. Recognize them as new materials driving a better outcome. They are also evidence that you are becoming a trusted advisor.

Each learning experience presents Hub Leaders with opportunities to adapt their approach and execution to this new data. The Hub Leader understands this and avoids the ego that resists change. Hub Leaders remain committed to the mission as planned on the one hand while being open to adaptation to potentially improved plans for work on the other hand.

The successful Hub Leader understands that the plans (how things get done) remain flexible to best meet the facts as they are known. Goals (what is to be done) are less flexible and are only changed if there are compelling changes in facts that merit a shift. Mission (why the work is being done) almost never changes. The Core Threads are woven into Operations because it is right thing to do for both customers and the business. That never changes.

Chapter 24

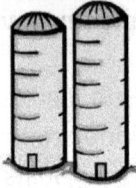

Go to Work

"You cannot dream yourself into a character; you must hammer and forge yourself into one."

- Henry David Thoreau

When all the thinking, planning, scheming, analyzing and talking is done, the last part of the work is ... work. It is then when Hub Leaders roll up their sleeves, put their heads down and go to work. This is the place where Hub Leaders begin to earn their stripes. This is where "gonna do" turns into "done, what's next." It's the place the Hub Leader's value begins to manifest.

In this last chapter we touch on a few points about how the Hub Leader works in the organization. Consider this the Hub Leader's treasure map providing a system of actions to navigate through the organization and among the silos.

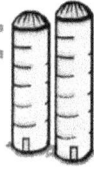

Resource Snapshot

Drive
Daniel H. Pink

Drive is an analysis of the new pattern to motivate self and team (Motivation 2.0). Pink discusses how the system of carrot (rewards) and stick (punishment) is no longer effective. In its place, Pink sets out a system of three elements: autonomy, mastery and purpose. Through this trio, motivation is deeper and more sustainable.

Key Quote
"Solving complex problems requires an inquiring mind and the willingness to experiment one's way to a fresh solution. . . . Only engagement can produce mastery."

Website
www.danpink.com/books/drive

Why this Resource?
The mission of a Hub Leader is a consistent progress of work over time. Sustainable motivation is required for the Hub Leader and team. Pink's book can help with that motivation.

www.silostopillars.com/resource-snapshot

Work Within the System

We all love the stories of the renegade, the lone wolf – that person who bucks the system and convinces everyone she is right, they are wrong and, in the end, wins the day. Those stories make great movies. They do not work well in real life.

Systems exist in an organization for various reasons. Some of those reasons are good. Others are not. The Hub Leader is not the best positioned to take on these systems and be a renegade.

Remember, the Hub Leader is already a heretic for the ideas being pursued. Plus, the Hub Leader presents a very real sense of disruption to Operations – the group that brings revenue to the organization. In short, the Hub Leader does not have the standing to buck the system.

As a Hub Leader, be a team player. Work within the system as it exists in the business. Be seen as someone who wants to strengthen the system, not mock it. Executive leaders give a Hub Leader more sway if there is no fear of upheaval or mutiny. You can look for opportunities to nudge the system in directions that make things better. But never make challenging the system your primary mode of work.

Work for the Organization's Good

Throughout the book we have touched on the Hub Leader's challenge to go from an outsider to an insider with Operations. We have talked about becoming a trusted advisor and protecting your credibility at all costs. This is never truer than when the Hub Leader is executing in the silos.

A key to remember about the work is that it is <u>always</u> for the customers' and organization's good. Hub Leaders are a bit of an evangelist in the work they do. They persuade those around them of the value the Core Threads work brings to the company for its customers.

To maintain legitimacy and credibility, that message must be based on the good of the company and its

customers. If there is any sense that the message is for the good of the Hub

> *Be seen as someone who wants to strengthen the system, not mock it.*

Leader, the Hub Leader suffers a significant setback.

Do your work for the company and its customers. You will be rewarded for the work you do. If not, there are plenty of companies who would love to have you transform their silos into pillars and serve their customers better.

Engage Guerrilla Tactics

At times, Hub Leaders should engage in guerrilla tactics. They should work around the edges; find resources who want to help in an "unofficial capacity." Guerrilla tactics create opportunities to move the needle more quickly and . . . they are fun!

Jay Conrad Levinson is the father of *Guerrilla Marketing*, a strategy of using low cost but effective avenues to market goods and services. *Guerrilla Marketing* focuses on "off the beaten path" strategies to position companies and brands on a level playing field with big name, highly resourced companies and brands. Levinson describes the core of *Guerrilla Marketing* this way:

> *I tell my clients that the single most important word for them to remember while they are engaged in marketing is commitment. It means that they are taking the marketing job seriously. They're not playing around, not expecting miracles. They have scant funds to test their marketing—they must act. Without commitment, marketing becomes practically impotent.*

Engaging in guerrilla tactics as a Hub Leader tests your commitment in the same way as *Guerrilla Marketing* tests the upstart company or brand.

As a Hub Leader, what are you willing to do to help your organization and your customers? Are you committed to your work as a Hub Leader enough to ensure there is passion in the plan and sweat in the work? Can you take small, calculated risks to do some important work outside the system? If so, you will find opportunities to use a few guerrilla tactics.

In the End, It's Just Work

Thomas Edison said, "Opportunity is missed by most people because it is dressed in overalls and looks like work." Being a Hub Leader requires a tremendous amount of work. At a minimum, it requires work on yourself, work in relationships and work on process.

Being a Hub Leader has times of difficulty and conflict. You may feel like you are not making progress. You may feel those around you pushing hard against you. You may also feel times of being ignored.

In all of these times, the most important thing to do is just keep working. Keep putting one foot in front of the other. Have one more conversation. Offer one more item of help. Why? Because in the end, it's just work.

Being a Hub Leader also brings times of profound pride and joy when the weaving produces positive customer interactions. There are also the occasions when your operational colleagues have the "Aha" moment and understand how the Core Threads strengthen what they are doing for customers.

In the beginning of the book you were challenged to become a Hub Leader, "if you chose." Reaching this point in the book and absorbing all the facets of how Hub Leaders transform silos into pillars, your choice seems obvious.

Go be a Hub Leader. Go weave Core Threads into Operations. Go transform silos into pillars. Go be the very best you can be.

A Personal Note

Thank you for taking this journey with me. I am sure you had a number of insights as you worked through this book. Some may have been when you saw things from a different perspective (thank you, Mr. Keating). Others may have been when you disagreed with my point entirely. No matter the cause, I hope you found value in the book and its ideas and, more importantly, it sparked ideas of your own.

Now is when the challenge begins. How do you take this book and turn yourself into your best Hub Leader? The best part of that answer is that it is uniquely defined by you. The worst part of the answer is that it is uniquely defined by you. There is no cookie-cutter. There are no absolutes. It all rests in your hands, brain and heart.

Look deeply and critically into your life -- personal and professional. Each of you has great contributions to make. Use this book as a call to unleash those contributions. The world needs you!

I wish you all the best as you grow into your best Hub Leader. Weave the Core Threads to bring value to your customers and success to your organization. If I can be of help, let me know.

Godspeed,

With Gratitude

We all are on a journey to be who we should be or do what we should do. Many help along that journey. Fortunately for me, this books gives me an opportunity to express publicly my gratitude to some of the key people who have helped me on my journey.

To my wife and best friend, Lydia who always pushes me to be who and what she sees in me. I Love You. To my Mom and Dad for whom there are simply not enough pages to thank you for the love you gave me and the opportunities you made possible.   To my big brother, Barney who has <u>always</u> had my back. To my friend, Steve Towers for listening, teaching and helping me capture the Hub Leader vision that sparked this book.   To my dear friend and mentor, Faye Caldwell for being honest (sometimes brutally) about what I needed (and continue to need) to do to achieve my dreams. To my buddy, Gary Jones who saw something in a baby law student nearly thirty years ago and has simply continued to give his friendship and wise counsel over these three decades. To Benn Sledge, my brother from another mother, an undying voice of support and optimism for me. To my colleagues, namely Dr. Heather Fehling and Patti Blackstaffe, who helped me craft this book into a useful tool for like-minded leaders.

To all the teachers, coaches and other leaders who each made their marks on my life. I appreciate all of you and thank you for what you have given me.

Resources

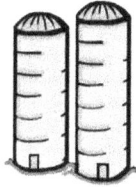

Tapestry Core is your oasis on the journey to and through Hub Leadership. Being a Hub Leader is challenging in so many ways. We want to be there for you to support your success. We also help organizations find their path from silos to pillars. Go to **TapestryCore.com** to learn more about how we can help, including:

- **Private Coaching**: Let us work with you to develop your tool kit to be a Hub Leader in your career.

- **Corporate Silo Transformation**: We work with companies to identify near term and long term opportunities to strengthen the organization by transforming silos to pillars.

- **Hub Leader Development**: We work with companies to identify high potentials who would benefit from adding Hub Leadership techniques to their skill set.

Visit **SilostoPillars.com** and **TapestryCore.com** regularly for explore our resources and other ways to connect.

@TapestryCore

www.TinyURL.com/TapestryCore